LIFE ALONG
THE DELAWARE BAY

LIFE ALONG THE DELAWARE BAY

Cape May, Gateway to a Million Shorebirds

Lawrence Niles · Joanna Burger · Amanda Dey

Photography by Jan van de Kam

with contributions from Kevin Kalasz · David Mizrahi · Humphrey Sitters

Rivergate Books

an Imprint of
Rutgers University Press

New Brunswick, New Jersey, and London

Library of Congress Cataloging-in-Publication Data

Niles, Larry.
    Life along the Delaware Bay : Cape May, gateway to a million shorebirds /
Lawrence Niles, Joanna Burger, and Amanda Dey ; photography by Jan van de Kam ;
with contributions from Kevin Kalasz, David Mizrahi, and Humphrey Sitters.
       p.   cm.
    Includes bibliographical references and index.
    ISBN 978–0–8135–5246–0 (hardcover : alk. paper)
    1. Shore birds—New Jersey—Cape May.   2. Shore birds—Delaware Bay (Del. and
N.J.)   3. Natural history—New Jersey—Cape May.   4. Natural history—Delaware Bay
(Del. and N.J.)   5. Cape May (N.J.)—Description and travel.   6. Delaware Bay
(Del. and N.J.)—Description and travel.   7. Shore birds—Conservation—New Jersey—
Cape May.   8. Shore birds—Conservation—Delaware Bay (Del. and N.J.)
9. Cape May (N.J.)—Environmental conditions.   10. Delaware Bay (Del. and N.J.)—
Environmental conditions.   I. Burger, Joanna.   II. Dey, Amanda.
III. Kam, Jan van de.   IV. Kalasz, Kevin.   V. Mizrahi, David, Ph.D.
VI. Sitters, Humphrey.   VII. Title.
    QL696.C48N56 2012
    598.3'30916346—dc23

                            2011023341

A British Cataloging-in-Publication record for this book is available from the British Library.

The views and conclusions contained in this publication are those of the authors and should
not be interpreted as representing the opinions or policies of the U.S. Government. Mention
of trade names or commercial products does not constitute their endorsement by the U.S.
Government.

Visit our Web site: http://rutgerspress.rutgers.edu

Manufactured in China

As sure as the shorelines of the Delaware Bay will change over time, so will the nature of man's reliance on the resource. *Life Along the Delaware Bay* beautifully documents centuries-old natural phenomena, and the intricate relationships that bring together a variety of species, including people. Each of us is challenged to ensure the region's wonders are sustained for future generations. The following sponsors care deeply about that future.

 Conserve Wildlife Foundation of New Jersey

 Citizens United to Protect the Maurice River and its Tributaries

 Sun National Bank

 National Park Service

 New Jersey Natural Lands Trust

May the great migrations of all creatures prosper on Delaware Bay and its shores.

Project Management: Bryce Schimanski
Design and Composition: Ellen C. Dawson
Copyediting: Alice Calaprice
Text typefaces: Dante, Helvetica Neue, and Tiepolo

Printed in China through Four Colour
Print Group, Louisville, Kentucky

Contents

Preface

Well over half of the people in the world live within one hundred miles of coasts, and the number is increasing rapidly. Thus, there is a great deal of interest in our coastal landscapes. People love to live, work, visit, and recreate in coastal areas. Coastal towns and villages teem with charm, history, and culture, and small bays and estuaries provide untold adventures for any naturalist. The Delaware Bay coastline itself is wild, yet home to old towns and villages, fishing piers and marinas, and a myriad of recreational and commercial fisheries. It is also home to one of the world's largest and most important migratory bird stopovers.

There are many books that focus on Chesapeake Bay, the New York/New Jersey harbor, and other coastal bays, but none that explores the unique treasure that is Delaware Bay. This book takes an ecosystem approach to understanding the species that live and migrate through Delaware Bay, which is, after Chesapeake Bay, one of the East Coast's largest and most diverse bays. Once ignored by both Delaware and New Jersey, the bay has become the focal point for a classic "commons" fight over resources. The migrant shorebirds need horseshoe crab eggs to put on enough weight to migrate north to their Arctic breeding grounds. Other marine species rely on young horseshoe crabs and their eggs for survival. Fishermen need female horseshoe crabs for bait. And birdwatchers stream to the bay to watch the spectacle of thousands of spawning horseshoe crabs and dense flocks of migrant shorebirds. The horseshoe crab is the keystone species, and the health of its populations has cascading effects on the other inhabitants of the bay.

The book focuses on Delaware Bay as an ecosystem, the horseshoe crab as a keystone species within that system, and the crucial role that the bay plays in the migratory ecology of the red knot, ruddy turnstone, sanderling, and semipalmated sandpiper. It also includes chapters on the culture, industries, and history of Cape May and Lewes, as well as migration, horseshoe crabs, other bird species, other important wildlife populations, and the threats to the bay ecosystem. We describe current efforts to protect the bay and what new efforts must take place to ensure that the bay remains an intact ecological system.

Our aim is to inform people who are interested in natural history, who support conservation activities, and who love the history and culture of the bay. We expect that the book will be especially useful for conservationists, ecologists, and political and policy professionals, as well as the general public, looking for guidance on bay-wide conservation. The book features lovely photographs that capture the essence of the bay and its wildlife, and insightful, beautiful essays by naturalists who are also scientists. We were striving to capture the beauty and majesty of this wild jewel that resides within easy driving distance of New York City, Philadelphia, and even Washington, D.C. We hope the book will be of interest to the nearly 50 million people of the mid-Atlantic states, many living within only a few hours' drive of the Delaware Bay. Ultimately, we hope (or pray?) that such familiarity with the bay's beauty and problems will lead to its protection for our grandchildren.

Lawrence Niles
Joanna Burger
Amanda Dey
Jan van de Kam

Delaware Bay, June 2011

Acknowledgments

Over the years an incredible number of dedicated biologists and volunteers have worked tirelessly to preserve and protect the shorebirds and other wildlife of Delaware Bay. From the very beginning a committed group of scientists (including the authors and contributors to this book) have contributed to the project, including Allan Baker, Patricia González, Clive Minton, Dick Veitch, Mark Peck, Ron Porter, Susan Taylor, Peter Fullagar, Jeannine Parvin, Steve Gates, Phil Atkinson, Graham Austin, Gregory Breese, Jacquie Clark, Nigel Clark, Simon Gillings, Rob Robinson, and Jean Woods.

Other key staff and volunteers include: Larissa Smith, assistant biologist and manager of volunteers at Shorebird Stewards for the Conserve Wildlife Foundation of New Jersey and the N.J. Division of Fish and Wildlife conservation officers, all of whom diligently protect shorebird foraging beaches and educate the public each spring; Nellie Tsipoura of the New Jersey Audubon Society and Citizen Science volunteers, who document the distribution and size of migratory shorebird populations in New Jersey; and David Mizrahi and Eric Stiles of the New Jersey Audubon Society, who have conducted significant research on Delaware Bay shorebirds and have been dogged advocates for their protection. The Delaware Coastal Program was instrumental in developing and promoting shorebird research and conservation in Delaware. In the end, it is impossible to name the hundreds of volunteers who have come to the bay each year to help protect and band the birds, educate the public, and patrol the beaches.

We are indebted to Citizens United to Protect the Maurice River and Its Tributaries Inc. for the main funding for this book, and to Jane Morton-Galetto, CU's president, for her support of both this book and shorebird work on the bay. We also thank the Conserve Wildlife Foundation of New Jersey and its executive director, Margaret O'Gorman, and the New Jersey Natural Lands Trust for providing additional funds and logistical support. The initial shorebird work on Delaware Bay was spearheaded and funded by the Endangered and Nongame Species Program, Division of Fish and Wildlife, and the New Jersey Natural Lands Trust of the New Jersey Department of Environmental Protection. In Delaware most funding came from the Delaware Department of Natural Resources Environmental Control. The two state agencies continue to provide the main support and protection for the shorebirds. Among the other key funders are the Manomet Center for Conservation Sciences, National Fish and Wildlife Foundation, U.S. Fish and Wildlife Service, National Oceanic and Atmospheric Administration, Wildlife Conservation Society, Geraldine Dodge Foundation, and the Neotropical Migratory Bird Conservation Act.

Field research requires permits from various governmental agencies and land owners, and we thank the following: the U.S. Bird Banding Laboratory, U.S. Fish and Wildlife Service, New Jersey Department of Environmental Protection, the Nature Conservancy, and the many residents of the Delaware bayshore who voluntarily observe beach closures every spring. Much of the understanding of shorebirds in Delaware Bay has also depended on work in wintering areas, particularly South America and Florida. We thank Patricia González in Argentina; Ines de Lima Serrano in Brazil; Jorge Jordan, Carmen Espoz, and Ricardo Matus in Chile; Nancy Douglas, Jannell Brush, and Amy Schwartzer in Florida; and David Newstead in Texas.

Additional funding for Joanna Burger's work has been provided by the U.S. Fish and Wildlife Service, the U.S. Environmental Protection Agency, U.S. Department of Energy, National Institute for Environmental Health Sciences, Trust for Public Lands, the Environmental and Occupational Health Sciences Institute, and Rutgers University. Additional funding sources for Lawrence Niles's work have included the U.S. Fish and Wildlife Service and the Florida Fish and Wildlife Commission.

We also thank Bruce E. Beans, our independent copyeditor, for his thoughtfulness and hard work, and our skillful mapmaker, Michael Siegel. Our special thanks also to Marlie Wasserman, director of the Rutgers University Press, for her encouragement and support, and to the entire RUP staff for improving the manuscript and making the process enjoyable.

Finally, the authors, photographer, and contributors thank our families and friends who have understood our passion for shorebirds and the Delaware Bay ecosystem. Our sometimes single-minded devotion has stolen time from them, and their support has been much appreciated.

LIFE ALONG THE DELAWARE BAY

1 CAPE MAY, GATEWAY TO THE DELAWARE BAY

Each fall, Cape May, the nation's oldest seaside resort, containing some of our country's finest examples of Victorian architecture, attracts thousands of birders to witness one of the world's most spectacular bird migrations. Witmer Stone, the founding member of the Delaware Valley Ornithological Club, first described Cape May as an important autumn stopover for songbirds and hawks in the late nineteenth century. His classic 1937 book, *Bird Studies at Old Cape May*, still resonates among birders, if only because the migration remains as robust as ever. In fact, over the years the list of species migrating through the cape to their southern wintering areas has actually grown. We now know that the peninsula is important for migrant hawks, songbirds, woodcocks, butterflies, and dragonflies. Millions of people have come to the cape to enjoy the sea, the architecture, the shops, the birds, and the beautiful flying insects.

The Cape May Lighthouse overlooks the Hawk Watch, where New Jersey Audubon Society has counted hawks to follow population trends since 1976.

Merlins (*left*) and juvenile peregrine falcons (*below*) are common coastal migrants that are often seen at the hawk watch. The majority of raptors flying through Cape May are juveniles. (Photos by Kevin T. Karlson)

Hawks also migrate through Cape May in the spring, but they are no threat to the northward migration of red knots and turnstones on Delaware Bay because most have departed before the shorebirds arrive. Cooks Beach provides an excellent place for people to watch shorebirds while remaining far enough away to reduce disturbance.

Little do they know that by heading just a few minutes to the north and west they can step back in time to a place that remains essentially as Stone described it. The peninsula is a tenuous bit of coastal marsh, forests, and fields nestled between the Atlantic Ocean and Delaware Bay. In particular, thousands of acres of forest, marsh, and farmland border the bay, with a large portion of it permanently protected and publicly accessible. Many of the same birds seen on the cape first pass through the bayshore's abundant and rich habitats and—before crossing the bay and continuing south—often return and work the shoreline nearly up to the upper bay when they encounter adverse winds or weather at the tip of the peninsula at Cape May.

Even during the fall and throughout the other seasons, the bayshore supports much more wildlife: wintering waterfowl, breeding bald eagles, marine turtles, otters—all the wildlife one would see in an intact wild area rooted in the productive soil and water of the mid-Atlantic Coast. And yet, abundant and diverse as the wildlife of the Delaware bayshore may be, all of it pales next to the bay's most enduring legacy: the annual spring breeding of horseshoe crabs and the migrating shorebirds that inextricably depend on the crabs. For eons, millions of horseshoe crabs have crawled from the depths of the Atlantic's continental shelf to breed and lay eggs on the bay's sandy beaches. At the same time as the crabs cobble the beaches, tens of thousands of shorebirds magically descend on the bay. Depleted from arduous journeys from as far away as Tierra del Fuego, the birds attempt to restore themselves by feasting on the fatty eggs. In a few weeks, the birds that have put on enough weight fly off to their Arctic breeding areas.

In this book, we will describe this natural wonder and more. We will explore the bay's many unique ecological relationships, its people, the threats to ecological stability, and the solutions and projects that will help secure the bay for our children and grandchildren. Most of all, we will celebrate this unique ecological gem that lies hidden in plain sight in the most densely populated section of the country.

Down by the Sea

Long before Cape May claimed the title as the oldest U.S. seaside resort, this town at the mouth of Delaware Bay served as a way station for New England whalers in the late 1600s. Eventually these blue-water whalers settled here. Working from small boats, they killed sperm and right whales wintering in the bay, pulling the carcasses ashore for meat, blubber, and oil. Then, by the late 1700s, stagecoaches brought the first visitors to the Atlantic shore to enjoy the ocean's "curative" waters. In the early 1800s, sailing vessels from Philadelphia and Baltimore began delivering tourists, who swam and ate the abundant seafood. Even at this early time they took horse-drawn cabs to Higbee Beach, which is now a state wildlife management area on the lower Delaware Bay.

In the 1820s, steamships replaced the sailing vessels, providing Cape May with a monopoly on ocean tourism because the ships were much faster than a stagecoach ride to Atlantic City and other resorts. That advantage was lost with the advent of train service to Atlantic City in the 1850s and, in 1863, to the cape. That train service to its rival up the coast caused Cape May to fall into a minor slump that culminated in a great fire in 1878 that consumed thirty-five acres of the town. Cape May's decision then to preserve the town's character as a smaller, scaled-down version of its pre-fire era—homes and businesses were built in Queen Anne, Gothic, and American bracketed styles—gave us the charming city we know today.

In Cape May's heyday in the early 1900s, thousands of tourists flocked to this seaside resort, filling the stately Victorian houses that lined the beaches. The popularity of Cape May City and other Atlantic coastal resorts overshadowed much smaller resorts on Delaware Bay. Less well known, similar mansions attracted people to Lewes, Delaware. (Historic photo from the collection of the Mid-Atlantic Center for the Arts, Cape May, New Jersey)

Declining Fortunes

Today the contrast between the vibrant cities of the Atlantic Coast and the forlorn, forgotten, and weather-ravaged communities of the Delaware bayshore could not be greater. It was not always this way. While the resorts along the Atlantic Coast were still isolated by a long stagecoach or steamboat ride, restaurants, hotels, and amusements flourished in the late 1880s in the bay towns of Sea Breeze and Fortescue. Thousands of summer tourists came by steamship from Philadelphia to restore themselves with the brisk breezes and fresh seafood. Simultaneously, the farms along both sides of Delaware Bay—among the nation's first to be settled—were producing abundant harvests of corn and wheat that fed the growing Philadelphia region. The vegetable farming that made New Jersey the Garden State was begun in the early 1900s by Italian immigrants resettling from the Pennsylvania coal-mining regions, and eventually attracted such renowned food processors as the H. J. Heinz and Campbell Soup companies.

But true wealth came from the water. In the 1800s, fishermen began "farming" oysters by growing spat, or young oysters, in the less saline portions of the upper bay to avoid predation from species like the oyster drill. These were then dredged and replanted in the more saline waters of the lower bay, where they matured three years later. With as many as eighty boxcars of oysters rolling daily out of Bivalve, N.J., alone, oysters brought immense wealth to Bivalve and other bayshore towns, including Port Norris and Mauricetown in New Jersey and Leipsic, Bowers Beach, and Little Beach in Delaware. Oysters also fueled a vibrant boat-building industry in Dorchester, Leesburg, and Greenwich, N.J.

Then, during the 1940s, the masts of sailing vessels were cut and fishermen began using diesel power to rake the bottom—the first of a number of assaults on oysters that included several parasite epidemics, which decimated oyster populations. Regrettably, today fishermen collect only a fraction of the two million oysters once harvested yearly from the bay.

Development of shore communities began when farmers cut sod to build dikes to drain marshes and control water to make the land usable for farming or to encourage the growth of salt hay, as this drawing of Newark Bay (*above*) illustrates. From the late 1800s, oysters were harvested for nearby markets in Philadelphia and New York City, and shipbuilding was an important industry—as illustrated by these 1920s photos of oyster schooners in the Maurice River and oyster packing operations (*below*). (Historic photos from Delaware Bay Museum, Bayshore Discovery Project)

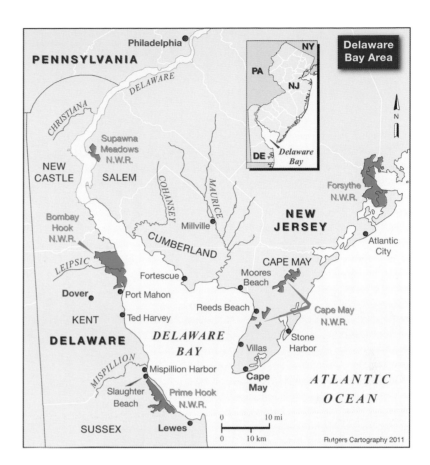

Map of Delaware Bay showing the key beaches where horseshoe crabs and shorebirds concentrate, as well as the major towns and cities, including Cape May Point. The narrow peninsula allows hawks, shorebirds, butterflies, and other migrants easy access to Atlantic coastal beaches, upland habitats, and the shores of Delaware Bay, making it one of the most important migratory habitats in the hemisphere.

Tidal swings in the creeks and rivers of Delaware Bay are an important influence on the invertebrates, shorebirds, and all other wildlife that depend on the bay ecosystem. Those photos show low tide at Money Island near Gandys Beach (*top*), and high tide six hours later (*bottom*) at the same location.

Shorebirds use all types of coastal wetland habitat for foraging and roosting, including the beaches and marshes of the Atlantic coast of New Jersey, such as the Forsythe National Wildlife Refuge north of Atlantic City. These marshes are especially important for shorebirds during fall migration.

5

Cape May's Critical Role in Fall Migration

On nearly any clear fall day with wind out of the northwest, you can find a cornucopia of migratory wildlife in Cape May and along the eastern shore of Delaware Bay. Hawks, songbirds, woodcocks, dragonflies, butterflies, and even owls concentrate on the Cape May peninsula, delighting thousands of visitors each year. The subject of scientific investigation for decades, the hawk migration is probably the best understood. Hawks, such as broad-winged, sharp-shinned, and Cooper's hawks, generally fly southwest toward their wintering areas. Pushed eastward by the prevailing autumnal northwest winds, they sometimes drift off course. Most adults will correct for the wind direction and fly along the ridges of the Appalachians, where they can be seen at places such as Hawk Mountain.

But the young don't make such adjustments, never knowing they will eventually struggle to stay over land as they approach the Atlantic Ocean. When they reach Cape May, they often stop over and replenish themselves, or wait for good conditions to cross the mouth of Delaware Bay. At the same time, songbirds, which mostly migrate at night, "fall out" of their high-altitude nocturnal flights to restore their energy with insects, berries, and a place to rest. They too end up in large numbers in Cape May—to the delight of tired and hungry hawks.

The flights of fall migrant hawks and songbirds mirror the spring flight of shorebirds, but also highlight the dramatic differences between these groups of species. Shorebirds stop over like other migrant birds, but in many fewer locations and for much longer periods. Most hawks and passerines stop each day to rest and restore their energy. Shorebirds may fly as long as six days without stopping and cover up to 5,000 miles. When they do stop over, they stop for at least a few days and, as they do on Delaware Bay, for as long as two to three weeks.

Like the hawks and songbirds, during such stopovers the shorebirds rest and restore themselves. But unlike these other migrants, the shorebirds often arrive with virtually no fat or energy reserves, so they must take far more time than hawks and passerines to build themselves back up for the next long leg of their flight.

Regardless, whether it functions as a brief autumnal pit stop for hawks and songbirds or a multiweek spring layover for shorebirds, Delaware Bay is a critical avian stopover.

There are many viewing opportunities for both the fall hawk migration at Cape May Point State Park (*above*), and the spring shorebird migration at the DuPont Nature Center at the Mispillion Harbor Reserve in Delaware (*below*). There is a hawk-watch tower at Cape Henlopen State Park, Lewes, Delaware, and there is a platform for viewing shorebirds at Reeds Beach in New Jersey.

The Delaware Bay (*left*) has only small wind-driven waves or flat, calm water, which are perfect conditions for spawning horseshoe crabs. In contrast, the Atlantic Ocean coast, here with a small group of dunlin feeding on beach invertebrates (*below*), has constant breaking surf that prevents crab spawning.

Shorebirds tend to fall into two groups in the spring stopover on the bay: those using the marsh and sod banks such as dunlins, short-billed dowitchers, and semipalmated sandpipers (*opposite*), and those using the bay beaches such as sanderlings, ruddy turnstones, and red knots (*shown here*).

The Atlantic Coast of New Jersey and Delaware attracts thousands of tourists each year to places such as Cape May with its historic Victorian architecture (*opposite, top*), Atlantic City, (*opposite, bottom, and left*) and Stone Harbor, where a flock of red knots, dunlins, black-bellied plovers, and other shorebirds roost (*below*). This economically important tourism also causes considerable disturbance to shorebirds, which can be alleviated with minor restrictions to beach use.

The true value of Delaware Bay to shorebirds comes from the massive spawn of horseshoe crabs that deposit billions of eggs on bay beaches (*opposite*). Shorebirds such as red knots consume these eggs in vast numbers in order to build up weight for their migration to their Arctic breeding grounds (*below*).

All over the bay, horseshoe crabs sometimes spawn in tremendous numbers, attracting many species of shorebirds such as these semipalmated sandpipers on Slaughter Beach, Delaware (*opposite, top*). The density of spawning crabs, however, varies greatly throughout the bay, leaving many shorebirds unable to find sufficient quantities of eggs (*opposite, bottom*). Sometimes, crab spawning is prevented by wind-driven waves that overturn crabs (*shown here*).

2 HORSESHOE CRABS

For most people, horseshoe crabs are odd creatures that look like they have just crawled from the bottom of the ocean. In fact they have, coming ashore once a year to breed on narrow ribbons of sand in coastal beaches from Maine to Mexico and elsewhere around the world. The crab is an ancient animal that has survived virtually unchanged for 445 million years. It emerged as a species before the separation of the continents as we know them now, 245 million years before dinosaurs and 442.5 million years before early humans. They have survived ice ages and meteor strikes that caused the mass extinction of most other species, yet they may not survive the effect of modern man.

Four species of horseshoe crabs occur around the world—two along the west coast of India (*Tachypleus gigas, Carcinoscorpius rotundicauda*); two along coastal Japan, Hong Kong, Taiwan, and Thailand (*Tachpleus tridentatus* and *C. rotundicauda*); and one along the U.S. Atlantic Coast and Mexico's Yucatan Peninsula (*Limulus polyphemus*). The U.S. horseshoe crab population is centered on Delaware Bay, which hosts the largest breeding concentration of horseshoe crabs in the world. Each spring on the highest tides, thousands of mature female crabs—a minimum of nine to ten years of age—come ashore multiple times, attended by several males, to lay eggs. The female excavates a pit near the tidal edge where she lays a cluster of 3,000 to 10,000 eggs; males release free-swimming sperm and fertilize the eggs before they are buried under six inches or more of sand. Spawning several times per season, females will lay up to 80,000 eggs a year. Wave action and the spawning activity of many horseshoe crabs bring buried eggs to the surface of the sand.

These are lost to the horseshoe crab population, but they are anything but wasted. They are eagerly consumed by the largest gathering of migratory shorebirds in the Western Atlantic Flyway in order to fuel their journey to Arctic breeding grounds.

In the 1950s, researchers found that the copper-based, blue-colored blood of horseshoe crabs quickly forms protective clots around bacteria—an extremely important discovery for human health. By 1970, Limulus Amoeboycte Lysate (LAL)—an extract of horseshoe crab blood cells—was approved by the Food and Drug Administration to test injectable drugs and medical devices for bacterial contamination. Next time you get a shot, receive stitches, or have surgery, thank horseshoe crabs for protecting you from infection.

The horseshoe crab is an ecological generalist that preys on marine worms, small clams and mussels, crustaceans, snails, and slugs. This and its superb immune system may have contributed to its staying power through millions of years of ecological calamity. But this helps no more. All four species of horseshoe crab are believed to be in moderate-to-serious decline. The Indo-Pacific populations have declined because coastal nursery and spawning habitats are being consumed by wetland reclamation

Primary Range of the Horseshoe Crab

— Limulus polyphemus
— Tachypleus tridentatus
— Tachypleus gigas*
— Carcinoscorpius rotundicauda*
*These two species share the same habitat

Rutgers Cartography 2011

Horseshoe crabs occur in the United States and Asia. Most of the U.S. spawning population, *Limulus polyphemus,* is in Delaware Bay. There are smaller numbers in estuaries along the East Coast from Maine to Florida, with significant numbers in Massachusetts and South Carolina.

Species closely related to *Limulus polyphemus* occur in Japan and Indonesia, where they are considered endangered. All horseshoe crab species are on the International Union for Conservation of Nature and Natural Resources (IUCN) red list.

Male and female horseshoe crabs can be distinguished by their size (females are larger) and by the pincer on the end of the front legs of males. Here a male has been overturned by the surf and struggles to right himself with his tail or telson. The slipper shells clinging to the shell indicate that this animal is probably old.

and degraded by water pollution (including heavy metals). They also are being overfished for food and other uses.

Similarly, the U.S. horseshoe crab population has declined due to coastal development, bulkheading, and beach hardening. The main population on Delaware Bay collapsed because of overharvesting by fishermen who use the crabs as bait to catch whelk (conch), minnows, and eels. Over 400,000 horseshoe crabs are taken for bait each year from the Delaware Bay breeding population. Most are taken at sea but many are still harvested off bay beaches. New Jersey has a moratorium on crab harvesting. Bleeding crabs for LAL can result in mortality of about 15 to 30 percent depending on the amount of blood taken, holding time, and conditions. The biomedical community releases crabs from where they were taken and is working to improve industry practices to reduce mortality. Losses from bait fisheries are compounded by the focus on bigger female crabs, which carry eggs. While fisheries agencies have heralded the success of harvest reductions over the last ten years, as of 2010 the Delaware Bay's adult horseshoe crab population had not yet shown signs of recovery.

Medical Use of Horseshoe Crab Blood

Since 1977, Limulus Amoebocyte Lysate (LAL) derived from horseshoe crab blood has become accepted worldwide for testing the safety of injectable drugs and medical implants. The LAL Test has essentially replaced the Rabbit Pyrogen Test (or "Rabbit Test") for detecting bacterial contamination. It does this by clotting immediately when it comes in contact with harmful bacteria called endotoxins.

Endotoxins are the most common fever-causing agents likely to be found in injectable drugs and on medical devices. They reside in the cell wall of bacteria, especially gram-negative bacteria that cause pneumonia, cholera, meningitis, respiratory infections, and a host of other diseases. As mammals, we ingest endotoxins all the time with no ill effect—our stomachs are full of gram-negative bacteria. However, if introduced into our bloodstream through wounds, inhalation, or medical procedures, endotoxins can cause severe infection.

Before LAL, the Rabbit Test was the standard. It requires injection of a substance into the blood or spinal fluid of a live rabbit and a waiting period of twenty-four hours or more to see if fever or symptoms of infection occur. The immediate detection of endotoxins by the LAL Test revolutionized our ability to protect the world's supply of injectable and intravenous drugs, vaccines, antibiotics, and medical devices, and to con-

A horseshoe crab struggles to right itself in the surf on a bay beach. Each day during the breeding period the surf overturns thousands of crabs. Most right themselves with their strong tails, others die and are eaten by gulls and other birds. More crabs overturn in strong onshore winds, which increase the height of surf. People sometimes walk beaches to right crabs, which saves the crabs, but the disturbance they cause stops birds from feeding and may force them to other less suitable locations.

trol endotoxins present in processes and equipment used to produce pharmaceutical products. For example, LAL is used to test high-purity water, which is essential to the manufacture of all drugs and the processing of medical devices.

Each year more than a half million horseshoe crabs from the Atlantic Coast population are bled for medical purposes. Mortality from bleeding may be contributing to a lack of signigicant increase in the crab population. Improvements in biomedical practices will also reduce crab mortality.

Researchers take egg samples from a bay beach to count the density of horseshoe crab eggs within two inches of the surface. The survey, led by Daniel Hernandez in New Jersey and Dick Weber in Delaware, creates a baywide index of egg densities based on numbers in cylindrical core samples.

Of the more than 148 miles of Delaware Bay coastline, only about a third is optimal for crab spawning; the rest is either of suitable quality, developed, or sod bank. Gently sloping sandy beaches with medium to coarse sand are best for spawning, but crabs will use many other types of beach to breed, including mud banks. Eggs laid in poor substrates usually don't hatch because of poor oxygenation.

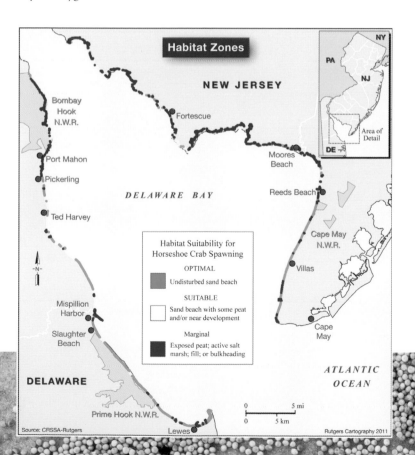

Importance of the Bay for Spawning Horseshoe Crabs

The bay is important to shorebirds because of horseshoe crab spawning, and the bay is critical for spawning crabs for several reasons. First, over its entire length the bay has a relatively shallow maximum depth of less than twenty feet. This allows bay water to heat up quickly in the spring to a critical threshold temperature of 15 degrees C or 59 degrees F, which stimulates crab breeding. Fortunately, but certainly not by accident, this onset of breeding coincides with the first arrivals of shorebirds from southern wintering areas. But the bay is also distinguished by the vast expanse of marsh and beach habitat available for spawning crabs. Of the bay's 148 miles of shoreline, more than 63 percent is potentially suitable for crab breeding and about a third is optimal for breeding. This large expanse results in the superabundance of crabs that is the backbone of the birds' stopover. Each spawning crab digs up and exposes the eggs of other spawners, thus making them readily available for the shorebirds. Prior to the overharvest of crabs in the 1990s, the eggs were so dense—as many as 100,000 per square yard—that shoreline waves created wrack lines thick with eggs that were easily devoured by shorebirds, gulls, and even fish.

A biologist holds an egg mass that includes up to 5,000 eggs. Female crabs start laying eggs when they are nine years old and come ashore to lay eggs multiple times each season.

A thin layer of horseshoe crab eggs coats the shoreline of a Delaware Bay beach (*below*). The variation in color relates to the age; freshly laid green eggs turn yellow as they mature.

A Keystone Species

The horseshoe crab is one of many invertebrates that live and breed in Delaware Bay. For many years, it was exploited without regard for its role in the bay ecosystem. Over time, we have come to realize that the horseshoe crab is a keystone species—a species with a unique role in supporting many other animals in the food web. Without keystone species, other species in the web may decline or collapse, causing cascading effects on even more animals. This is certainly true of horseshoe crabs in the Delaware Bay.

Horseshoe crab eggs and young are eaten by small fish, eels, and the endangered loggerhead turtle, as well as a wide range of birds, including shorebirds, gulls, and egrets. In turn, small fish are eaten by larger fish. Horseshoe crab eggs and young have been found in the stomach of many Delaware Bay species, from weakfish to glossy ibis. Adult crabs are also prey for sea turtles. In addition, horseshoe crabs are used as bait to catch eels, minnows, and common whelk (or conch), creating an opportunity for people to make a living.

But this desirable bait is also the cornerstone of the bay's tourism industry, which attracts bird watchers, nature lovers, and photographers. There is nothing like seeing a mass of spawning horseshoe crabs pitch and roll in the surf on a full-moon high tide and throngs of migrant shorebirds eagerly feeding on crab eggs on the following morning's tide.

A tagged male horseshoe crab attempts to breed on a bay beach among a group of red knots, ruddy turnstones, dunlins, semi-palmated sandpipers, and sanderlings, while a herring gull looks on (*above*). Biologists with the U.S. Fish and Wildlife Service and New Jersey and Delaware fish and wildlife agencies lead tagging programs to understand long-range movements and mortality rates. To report tags, people can call 1-888-LIMULUS.

Dunlin feed on horseshoe crab eggs exposed by a horseshoe crab that has just spawned. Most eggs consumed by shorebirds are a result of the high density of crabs on Delaware Bay. While digging their own hole to lay eggs, female crabs unearth egg masses laid by other females.

Several other species, such as this boat-tailed grackle (*left*), feed on horseshoe crab eggs.

Horseshoe crabs were once much more abundant than today. Historically, crabs were used as fertilizer until commercial, petroleum-based fertilizers became available in the 1940s. As these photographs from 1924 at Bowers Beach, Delaware, illustrate, incredible numbers of crabs were harvested off the beaches and then stacked for processing. (Photo from Delaware State Archives)

A Long History of Overharvesting

Horseshoe crabs make good bait because they are easy and inexpensive to collect. Historically, when they were cheap and abundant, horseshoe crabs were ground up for use as fertilizer. More recently Delaware baymen used horseshoe crabs to catch eels—often used as bait for striped bass—and minnows, which are used as bait for many other sport fish. The current overharvest of horseshoe crabs was triggered by the collapse of fish stocks on the New England Coast. Desperate for new species to harvest, fishermen found new value in the common whelk, which was being sold in overseas markets. The problem was that they needed cheap and accessible bait. In the early 1990s, trucks from New England started arriving on the Delaware Bay to pick up horseshoe crabs breeding on the beaches and haul them away. It didn't take long for other fishermen of the Atlantic to learn the newfound value of whelk, and before long the harvest of horseshoe crabs had dramatically increased. From 1992 to 1997 the harvest grew from less than 100,000 to over 2.5 million annually. At the time, horseshoe crab populations were only roughly estimated at somewhere between 4 million and 18 million crabs.

Compounding the overharvesting problem is the fishermen's predilection for female crabs; their eggs make them especially attractive bait for eels and minnows. Harvesting breeding-age animals that take nine or ten years to sexually mature is more like mining—it is a short-lived enterprise. By the early 2000s, the horseshoe crab population had crashed and eggs that were available on the beach surfaces to shorebirds had all but disappeared.

Current estimates of the horseshoe crab population still vary widely, but the U.S. Geological Survey estimates the Delaware Bay spawning population at approximately 6 million females and 13 million males. The bay spawning population winters offshore from New Jersey, Delaware, Maryland, and Virginia. Excluding New Jersey, the current harvest taken totals about 330,000 per year, or about 2 percent of the estimated population. Fishermen have pursued many different ways to reduce the need for so many crabs, including using one female for two traps, increasing the use of males, and developing bait bags.

Male horseshoe crabs cluster around single females during sunset on Reeds Beach, New Jersey (*opposite*). Shorebirds often forage for eggs among breeding crabs, including a somewhat desperate red knot picking eggs off a female horseshoe crab that has a male attached to her (*above*).

Crabs spawn on Reeds Beach, New Jersey, on two different days during a daytime high tide. Notice how the higher waves on the *left* reduce spawning density. Breeding density varies by water temperature, wind-driven wave height, and the time of high tide; spawning is always greatest during the night (*opposite*).

Gulls feed on windrows of horseshoe crab eggs blanketing Reeds Beach. This scene was once common throughout the bay when surface egg densities averaged more than 100,000 eggs per square yard—much higher than the current 5,000 eggs per square yard average. Obviously, shorebirds can quickly gain weight by foraging such windrows.

Laughing gulls forage among spawning horseshoe crabs on a vegetated bay beach. The vegetation on this beach impedes spawning by preventing crabs from digging. These partially sandy or muddy beaches comprise a significant portion of the bay's beaches.

Sandy beaches are better for spawning,
but wave action overturns thousands of crabs.

3 THE MOST IMPORTANT STOPOVER OF THE WESTERN HEMISPHERE

Walking along the Delaware Bay waterline under the light of a full moon in mid-May, you find yourself surrounded by horseshoe crabs having sex. The water is a frothy brew of crabs, crab eggs, and mucky sand that, by the following dawn, has settled into an all-you-can-eat buffet for red knots, ruddy turnstones, sanderlings, semipalmated sandpipers, and many other species of Arctic-nesting shorebirds. Over the course of an entire month, female horseshoe crabs accompanied by males repeatedly come ashore on most of the bay's sandy beaches and creek mouths, dig holes, and lay their eggs. This bonanza of food attracts shorebirds to one of the most important stopover areas in the world.

Shorebirds make stopovers along all the world's flyways, and Delaware Bay is one of the most important. Other major stopover sites include the Yellow Sea on the Australia-Siberia flyway, the Wadden Sea in the Africa–northern Europe flyway, and the Copper River Delta in Alaska. In each of these places, thousands upon thousands of shorebirds gather to make use of an abundant food source such as the horseshoe crab eggs in Delaware Bay. Prior to its decline, Delaware Bay hosted the largest number of individuals and species of shorebirds. But the unforeseen consequences of the overharvest of horseshoe crabs led to a decline in both abundant horseshoe crab eggs and then in shorebirds. The future of Delaware Bay as a key stopover depends upon restoring the population of horseshoe crabs.

Imagine that Delaware Bay is a dinner table set for friends who are weary and hungry after a long journey. Just as eggs start building up on the shore of the bay, shorebirds converge on the bay from all over the Western Hemisphere. Prior to the overharvest, biologists estimated more than 1.5 million shorebirds were stopping on the bay, making it one of the four most important shorebird stopovers in the world. From the diminutive least sandpiper to the gigantic whimbrel, at least fifteen species of shorebirds use the Delaware bayshore. While on the bay, species such as the red knot, ruddy turnstone, and sanderling can double their body weight with fat reserves that will fuel their flight to their Arctic breeding grounds.

A semipalmated plover pulls a marine worm from wet mud. Most shorebird species coming to the bay rely on horseshoe crab eggs to build weight quickly. But they also feed on other prey, such as mussels, mussel spat, marine worms, *Donax* species clams, and other marine invertebrates.

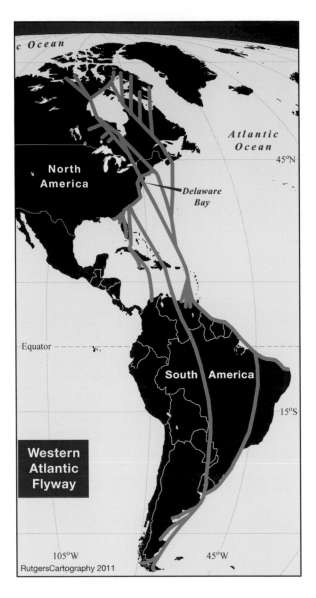

Western Atlantic Flyway

RutgersCartography 2011

The West Atlantic Flyway: In the past, migrant shorebirds were thought to follow shorelines, but recent research shows that they frequently make direct crossings over thousands of miles of unsuitable habitat. Flying north from Argentina, they may cross both the Amazon rain forest and the Atlantic Ocean in a single flight. When departing from Delaware Bay they head north–northwest straight across Canadian forests to the Arctic.

Joanna Burger from Rutgers University extracts a red knot from a cannon net catch at Reeds Beach while the rest of the catch team covers the net to minimize disturbance and heat stress. Both speed and care are essential to ensure the safety of the birds.

The flight to the Arctic from Delaware Bay is no big deal for a shorebird; it is only about 1,500 miles and we know that red knots are capable of flying up to 5,000 miles, as one did in 2010 when it flew nonstop from southern Brazil to North Carolina in six days. But the resources the birds acquire in Delaware Bay are not just for the flight, they are also needed to sustain them after arrival (when Arctic food resources are scarce) and to ensure that they are in good enough condition to breed successfully.

Most shorebirds arrive in Delaware Bay after long flights that deplete nearly all of their reserves. Researchers have captured some newly arrived red knots that were so thin that they were 40 grams, or 30 percent, below their normal fat-free weight of 133 grams (4.6 oz.). When they leave the bay, some knots can weigh as much as 240 grams, or 80 percent above their fat-free weight. These incredible weight gains over as little as two weeks are only possible because horseshoe crab eggs are energy-rich and easily digested, so the shorebirds can build up weight quickly and move out.

Horseshoe crabs not only provide the migrant shorebirds with an abundant food supply, but the impeccable timing of the spawn makes it available exactly when it is needed. Shorebirds must avoid arriving too soon in the Arctic because the frozen tundra is devoid of food, but if they get there too late they will not have time to breed successfully and the young will face adverse weather conditions before they can fledge and leave for their southern wintering areas. The best time to lay eggs in the Arctic is mid-June, so engorging themselves on enough fatty horseshoe crab eggs so they can leave the bay by early June is critical for successful breeding—and their continued survival.

Red knots, sanderlings, and ruddy turnstones search for scarce horseshoe crab eggs in depressions initially excavated by ruddy turnstones.

When shorebirds are densely packed, like this flock of red knots, leg flags are more difficult to read. Observing such banded birds has given scientists a greater understanding of the role of individual behavior within flocks.

BOOM! Catching Shorebirds with a Cannon Net

Much of what we know about the shorebirds that use the Delaware Bay stopover comes from catching them. Two methods are used: mist nets and cannon nets. Mist nets are nearly transparent, small-mesh nets strung upright on poles in the marsh. Shorebirds, like semipalmated sandpipers, cannot see the nets and get entangled when they fly into them. Cannon nets, which cover the area of a small house (30 feet by 70 feet), are attached to projectiles launched by two or three cannons charged with black powder. Within a millisecond, a net can be deployed over a flock of shorebirds and capture as many as three hundred birds in a single firing. This kind of power can be dangerous to both birds and humans. Rigid procedures are followed to ensure safety throughout the process. After a net is fired, a well-trained team moves quickly to the net and covers it and the birds with a lightly-woven shade-cloth to keep the birds calm. At the same time, the team erects burlap keeping cages constructed so the birds can move freely in a well-aerated and darkened space. This reduces the stress of captivity. Back at the net, the team carefully removes the birds and puts them in carrying boxes for transport to the keeping cages. Within minutes, the birds are safe, calm, and cool, and the team can start banding, weighing, and measuring them.

A flock of sanderlings (foreground) and red knots, just landing to forage, with spawning horseshoe crabs. These large concentrations of shorebirds give researchers excellent opportunities to study long-distance migration and the importance of shorebird stopovers.

The authors and their research team set a cannon net on Delaware Bay. The cannon net is seventy-five feet long and thirty feet wide, and is camouflaged by digging it into the sand. Three cannons are loaded with gunpowder and set at the correct angle to avoid injuring birds when the net is deployed. Fired over a flock of shorebirds, the net covers them within milliseconds. The team moves quickly to lift the birds out of the water onto dry ground, where they are covered to prevent injury and stress.

A Laboratory on the Beach

Each year scientists and volunteers come from Canada, Europe, South America, Australia, New Zealand, Asia, and Africa to help New Jersey and Delaware biologists work on captured shorebirds. After catching and securing the birds, the next job is banding. Each bird is fitted with a permanent metal band bearing a unique engraved number. On the upper leg, each bird is fitted with a lime-green colored leg flag inscribed with a unique, three-digit, alphanumeric code that can be seen from fifty yards away with a spotting scope. The flags have proved to be a big success because field identification of individual birds can be performed anywhere, anytime for many years without ever having to catch them again. The ease of collecting large amounts of data on marked birds with spotting scopes allows biologists to track the survival of marked birds from year to year and estimate population size. Biologists use different colored flags to identify the country in which each bird was banded: white for Canada, blue for Brazil, orange for Argentina, and red for Chile. After banding, birds are measured and weighed.

The declining weight of shorebirds in Delaware Bay in late May was the key to discovering the cause of the collapse of the Delaware Bay stopover. After years of catching birds and collecting weight data, biologists could say with certainty that there were not enough horseshoe crabs eggs for the birds to gain sufficient weight for their flight to the Arctic and for laying eggs. Tying together shorebird weights and flag resightings, biologists proved birds were dying faster than they were being replaced. In this way, the crash of red knot numbers was linked to the collapse of the horseshoe crab population.

Lawrence Niles reads the number of the U.S. Fish and Wildlife Service metal band on a bird previously banded in Delaware Bay. This bird, like all shorebirds banded on both sides of Delaware Bay, has also been fitted with a lime-green flag with a unique combination of letters and numbers that enables researchers to identify this bird at a distance of more than 150 feet.

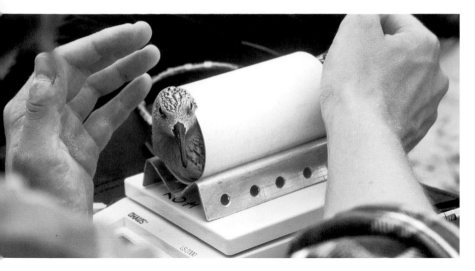

Captured birds are placed in a plastic tube to be weighed. The weight data proved pivotal in the controversy over horseshoe crab harvesting because it demonstrated that the loss of horseshoe crab eggs directly impacted the weight gain of shorebirds and their subsequent survival.

Wing and beak length are measured for all captured shorebirds to determine body size. Size measurements are critical to understanding a bird's condition in the same way that a big-boned person will weigh more than a small-boned person with the same relative fat level.

After birds are captured, they are placed in burlap keeping cages that allow free movement of air and have sufficient space for the birds to move around; the cages are also dark, which helps to keep the birds calm. Researchers then work in groups to process the birds (band, measure, and weigh them) as quickly and efficiently as possible. *Below*, a research team led by Kevin Kalasz from the Delaware Division of Fish & Wildlife processes a catch of red knots and ruddy turnstones near Bowers Beach, Delaware. Each team member is given a specific job: banding, measuring, weighing, or recording.

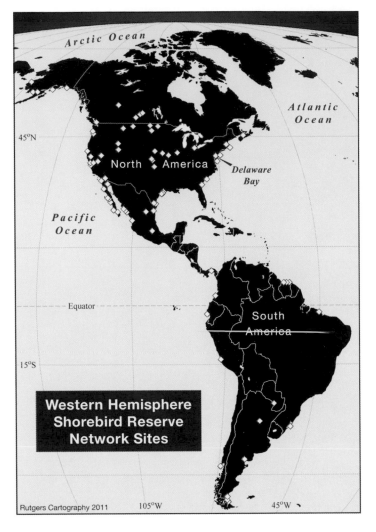

Major shorebird stopover sites are recognized by the Western Hemisphere Shorebird Reserve Network (WHSRN), but continuing research is identifying other important sites that need to be protected.

These foraging red knots include two banded birds. The bird on the left with a lime green flag had a VHF transmitter antenna attached on a Virginia beach by a banding team from Virginia Tech led by James Fraser. The bird on the right with a red leg flag had previously been captured in Tierra del Fuego, Chile.

Below, Mark Peck, from the Royal Ontario Museum in Canada, uses a telescope to read the leg flags of shorebirds at Kimbles Beach, New Jersey. Considerable effort is devoted each spring to read flags to understand migratory patterns and survival rates.

A sanderling (*left*) and a red knot, both in full breeding plumage, rest after foraging on Delaware Bay. These plump birds are nearly ready to leave the bay for their Arctic breeding grounds.

Why Do Shorebirds Depend on Stopovers?

Arctic-nesting birds have differing strategies for dealing with winter. Ptarmigan stay the winter while snow geese fly far enough south to reach unfrozen bays, like the Chesapeake and Delaware. Arctic-nesting shorebirds make long journeys to warmer climes. Along the way, they rely on stopovers that provide reliable food and safe roosts. In spring, shorebirds in the West Atlantic Flyway face a tight schedule and make long, nonstop flights between stopovers like San Antonio Oeste in Patagonia, Lagoa do Peixe in Brazil, and the Delaware Bay. There they stay for perhaps two to four weeks to restore themselves and gain additional resources to enable them to complete their migration to the Arctic. The Arctic breeding season represents only a short window of opportunity, so the birds must finish breeding and head south by early August, before winter closes in. Shorebirds also make long-distance, nonstop flights during their southbound migration. For example, in 2009 a red knot fitted with a geolocator device flew six days without stopping from Cape Cod, Massachusetts, to northern Brazil.

Clearly, high-quality stopovers on north- and southbound migrations are critical to survival. What makes a good stopover? Reliable, abundant, energy-rich foods and safe roost sites. While species may differ in their food preferences—semipalmated sandpipers foraging on mud flats for marine worms, red knots foraging on sandflats for clams and mussels—Delaware Bay is special because it provides seasonally abundant horseshoe crab eggs that are eagerly consumed by all species. Safe roosting places close to such food is the other essential characteristic of a good stopover site. The best roost sites are wide open spaces such as long, broad beaches and sandy islands where shorebird flocks rest safely because they can easily see approaching predators.

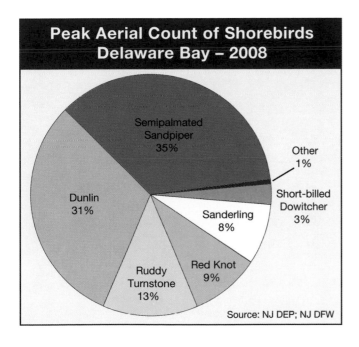

Peak Aerial Count of Shorebirds Delaware Bay – 2008

Semipalmated Sandpiper 35%

Dunlin 31%

Ruddy Turnstone 13%

Red Knot 9%

Sanderling 8%

Short-billed Dowitcher 3%

Other 1%

Source: NJ DEP; NJ DFW

Up to fifteen shorebird species can be found in the Delaware Bay each spring, but most are just eight species, and over half are semipalmated sandpipers and dunlins. Total shorebirds numbers have declined dramatically, from nearly half a million birds in the 1980s to fewer than 150,000 in 2010—according to aerial counts led by Kathy Clark of the N.J. Division of Fish and Wildlife.

Two turnstones in the Canadian Arctic (*left*), obviously recent arrivals due to their plump condition, forage in ice-covered tundra. The extra fat resources they carry will help ensure their survival until the ice melts and the abundant Arctic food supply becomes available.

A dense flock of red knots with sanderlings and
ruddy turnstones flush due to a disturbance.
When forced to leave their preferred feeding
sites, shorebirds burn up valuable energy moving
about the bay searching for undisturbed beaches.

38

Dunlins and short-billed dowitchers, which normally feed in bay marsh, sometimes feed on the bayshore. This creates even greater competition with shorebirds that primarily feed on the bayshore, including red knots, ruddy turnstones, and sanderlings, as well as laughing gulls.

39

40

Short-billed dowitchers (*opposite, top left*) and dunlin (*opposite, bottom left*) are less reliant on horseshoe crab eggs than species such as red knots, ruddy turnstones, and sanderlings (*below*), but eggs still account for at least half their diet while in the bay.

41

After accumulating sufficient fat resources, red knots fly to their Arctic breeding grounds, which are often covered with snow and ice—preventing them from feeding and underscoring the importance of the Delaware Bay stopover as a refueling source. Birds that fail to accumulate sufficient resources die en route or fail to breed. Shorebirds that succeed in securing a territory and a mate typically lay a clutch of four eggs (*inset*).

4 RED KNOTS

In 2009 a team of shorebird biologists, including this book's authors, caught a red knot on Delaware Bay with a cannon-powered net. They fitted it with both a colored flag emblazoned with the code "Y0Y" and a small device called a geolocator. The device does not transmit information, but records location data that, if the bird is recaptured, can provide biologists with an understanding of the bird's daily movements for a year or more. Following its release, over the course of the next twelve months the bird flew from Delaware Bay to the Canadian Arctic to breed; flew south to winter in Argentina; and then returned to Delaware Bay, where the bird was recaptured and fitted with a new geolocator. In just one year Y0Y had flown 17,236 miles.

This one bird tells us much of what we need to know about the New World red knot. It is an intrepid traveler that—relying on just a few important stopovers along the way—will overcome any number of problems to reach its breeding and wintering areas. There are three main populations of American red knot, each defined by the area in which it winters: the southeastern United States, northern Brazil, and Tierra del Fuego in Chile and Argentina. Prior to the population declines that started in the mid-1990s, total numbers exceeded 100,000 birds.

Red knots from all three wintering populations breed in the archipelago of arctic islands to the north and northwest of Hudson Bay. Most stop in Delaware Bay to refuel during northward migration, though some prefer the barrier islands of Virginia. Although the average red knot arrives in Delaware Bay at about 120 grams (4.2 oz.) and leaves at about 180 grams (6.3 oz.), individuals have arrived as low as 84 grams and departed at 244 grams. Clearly these birds don't worry about their weight, since some become so heavy they can barely lift off from the ground.

The mechanism for making this rapid transformation in body condition is a miracle of nature. Prior to making long-distance flights, the red knot begins to reduce the size of all its organs of digestion. Who needs a big stomach when you are flying nonstop for days? At the same time they increase the size of their organs and muscles necessary for flight, such as their heart, lungs, and wing muscles. Like Transformer toys, after a long flight the knots then transform again back to their normal condition.

This amazing physiologic transformation underpins these birds' extremely long migrations and underscores the extraordinary importance of the places where red knots stop over to regain their energy. Back in the 1980s researchers such as Brian Harrington and Guy Morrison studied the migration of the red knot. They discovered a number of places where knots congregate, and many of those same places are still important today—Bahia Lomas in Chile, San Antonio Este in Argentina, Lagoa de Peixe in Brazil, Florida's Gulf Coast, and, of course, Delaware Bay. It was not until 1981 that the true importance of Delaware Bay for shorebirds was established; then in 1986 the bay was designated the first "stopover of hemispheric importance" as part of a new shorebird conservation program, the Western Hemisphere Shorebird Reserve Network. WHRSN, a program of the Manomet Center for Conservation Sciences in Manomet, Massachusetts, now includes eighty-seven other sites stretching from Arctic Canada to the very tip of South America.

Although there are still many uncertainties about red knots in the West Atlantic Flyway, even after three decades of intensive work, one thing is certain—the availability of an abundant supply of horseshoe crab eggs in Delaware Bay is absolutely essential to their future well-being. During the 1980s, aerial counts in the bay regularly topped 90,000 knots. But then, as fishermen overharvested horseshoe crabs and the density of their eggs declined, the number of knots and all other shorebirds dropped. The red knot count fell to 50,000 in 2000, to 30,000 in 2004, and now averages around 16,000.

Except when they are in the Arctic, knots feed mostly on shellfish, which are swallowed whole and crushed in their strong guts. However, when the knots arrive in Delaware Bay with reduced-sized guts, they cannot feed on shellfish, which is why the energy-rich, easily digested horseshoe crab eggs are such a valuable food resource. Studies have shown that with the reduced egg supply it is advantageous for the knots to arrive early on Delaware Bay. Those that do, still have enough time to find the food they need. But invariably many arrive late and it is these birds that have suffered most. The decline in the food supply has led to a decline in the knots' average departure weight, and it has been found that lower departure weights lead to higher mortality.

Researchers estimate that, even if the horseshoe crab population is restored quickly, it may take over twenty years for the red knot population to recover.

Red knots were named for their brilliant red breeding plumage (*above*), but as they migrate south from their Arctic nesting areas they become all gray and white (*left*), a nondescript plumage that makes them hard to distinguish from many other shorebirds.

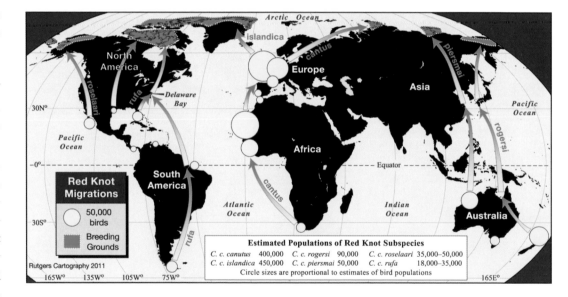

Red Knot Migrations

○ 50,000 birds

■ Breeding Grounds

Rutgers Cartography 2011

Estimated Populations of Red Knot Subspecies

C. c. canutus 400,000	*C. c. rogersi* 90,000	*C. c. roselaari* 35,000–50,000
C. c. islandica 450,000	*C. c. piersmai* 50,000	*C. c. rufa* 18,000–35,000

Circle sizes are proportional to estimates of bird populations

There are six subspecies of the red knot. All breed in the Arctic, but migrate along different flyways. The New World red knot (*Calidris canutus rufa*) migrates southward from the central Canadian Arctic to the northeast Atlantic Coast and then flies either directly to northern Brazil and Tierra del Fuego in South America or to wintering areas around Florida and the Caribbean islands. A second North American subspecies (*C. c. roselaari*) breeds in the Alaskan Arctic and flies along the Pacific Coast to Mexico. A third North American subspecies (*C. c. islandica*) breeds in the northeast Canadian Arctic and winters in the North Sea estuaries of England and the Netherlands. A European subspecies (*C. c. canutus*) breeds in the Russian Arctic and winters in Africa. The final two subspecies (*C. c. piersmai* and *C. c. rogersi*) breed in the Russian Arctic and migrate along the Asian Pacific coast to wintering areas in Australia and New Zealand.

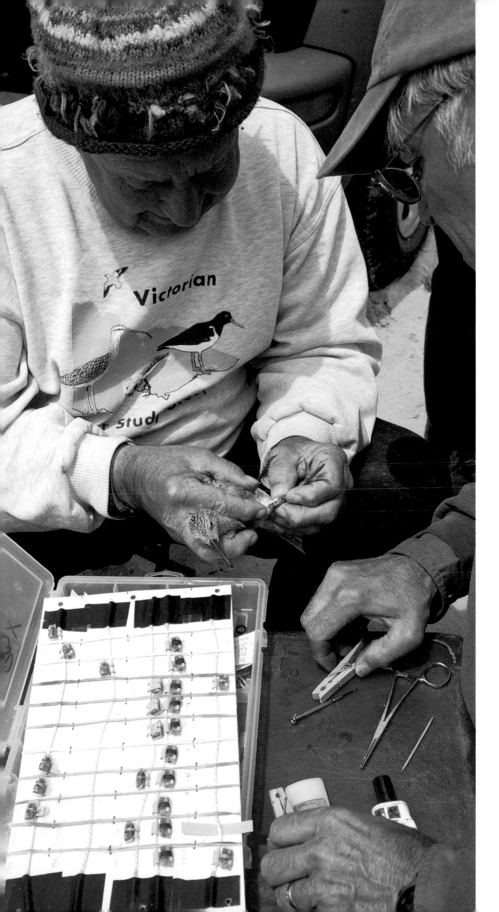

Using Geolocators to Track Red Knots

Technological innovations have transformed the study of shorebirds. Very High Frequency (VHF) radio transmitters have been used for decades, but their short transmission range makes them unsuitable for tracking shorebirds during long-distance migrations. Satellite transmitters are increasingly used for large shorebirds, such as bar-tailed godwits and whimbrels, but they are too heavy for small shorebirds, including most of those that frequent Delaware Bay. In 2009 biologists experimented with a tiny new device called a light-sensitive geolocator. Weighing about one gram, these devices do not transmit a signal. Instead, they record and store light levels—the time of dawn and dusk—daily for a year. These data allow a bird's daily position to be estimated with average accuracy of within 100 miles, which is more than adequate for studying the movements of a long-distance migrant such as the red knot. The main drawback of geolocators is that the birds must be recaptured in order to retrieve the data.

In May 2009 Larry Niles, Joanna Burger, and other researchers attached geolocators to forty-seven red knots in Delaware Bay. A year later three of these birds were recaptured and the location data were downloaded. The output showed that in late May 2009 they had all flown from Delaware Bay to the Arctic. In August they headed south. Two made long flights to northern Brazil, one fighting tropical storms over the Atlantic Ocean for several days. The third flew to southern Argentina where it spent the winter. In the spring of 2010 this bird made an amazing nonstop 5,000-mile flight from southern Brazil, over the Amazon and the Atlantic Ocean, to make landfall in North Carolina. It arrived on the bay a full year after it left. This was the longest nonstop flight ever recorded for a red knot, and one of the longest known flights of any species.

Clive Minton and Ronald Porter attach a geolocator, a small device that records information on the time of dawn and dusk that helps determine the bird's daily location.

A close-up view of a geolocator that has just been fitted to a red knot. The lime-green leg flag Y3V allows the bird to be identified as an individual by using a telescope.

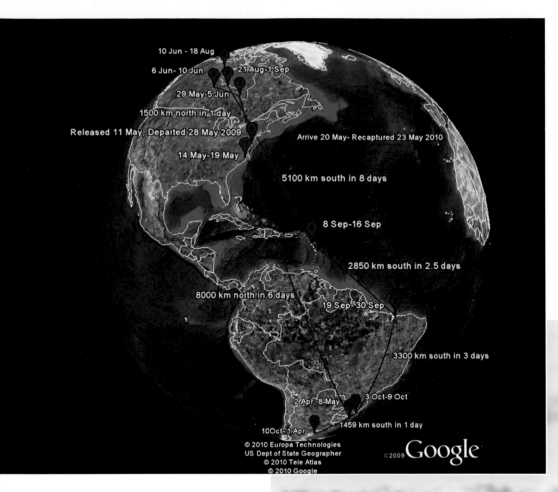

10 Jun - 18 Aug
6 Jun - 10 Jun
21 Aug - 1 Sep
29 May - 5 Jun
1500 km north in 1 day
Released 11 May, Departed 28 May 2009
Arrive 20 May - Recaptured 23 May 2010
14 May - 19 May
5100 km south in 8 days
8 Sep - 16 Sep
2850 km south in 2.5 days
8000 km north in 6 days
19 Sep - 30 Sep
3300 km south in 3 days
2 Apr - 8 May
3 Oct - 9 Oct
10 Oct - 1 Apr
1459 km south in 1 day

© 2010 Europa Technologies
US Dept of State Geographer
© 2010 Tele Atlas
© 2010 Google
©2009 Google

Map showing the migration route of a red knot fitted with a geolocator; it was named Y0Y for the flag that it carried on its leg. It left Delaware Bay on May 28, 2009, and returned to the bay almost a year later on May 20, 2010. From Delaware Bay it had migrated to its Arctic breeding area on Southampton Island, going through Churchill, Manitoba, on Hudson Bay. Leaving the Arctic on August 20, it flew past Cape Cod, Massachusetts, 2,000 miles to the Lesser Antilles. Then, after a week it flew on to the north coast of Brazil, where it stayed for 11 days. From there, it flew to Argentina, where it wintered for 173 days. After flying to the Brazil/Uruguay border it made one of the most amazing bird flights ever recorded, flying for 6 days and 3,000 miles nonstop to North Carolina's Outer Banks. Still carrying its geolocator, a few days later it arrived in Delaware Bay ready to refuel on horseshoe crab eggs.

The red knot with flag Y0Y feeds on crab eggs the day before it was recaptured with a cannon net on Delaware Bay. This bird's geolocator recorded the longest flight ever for a red knot (see map, above).

Red knot probing for horseshoe crab eggs in Delaware Bay.

Red knots in winter plumage, in Tierra del Fuego at the tip of South America, feed with a Hudsonian godwit (background). Throughout most of the year, knots feed mainly on bivalves (clams and mussels). Only on Delaware Bay do they feast on horseshoe crab eggs. In the Arctic they feed on small terrestrial and marine invertebrates. The knots' sensitive bills are also sensitive to pressure, allowing them to locate prey before they touch it. They always swallow prey whole, so size limits the foods that are available to them.

In brilliant red breeding plumage, red knots roost in a dense flock in Stone Harbor, New Jersey, just prior to their departure for the Arctic. While some birds sleep, others are alert or preening, which is characteristic of any flock of roosting shorebirds.

There is a sharp contrast between the red knot *below,* which is a slim, low-weight, recent arrival (and also paler in color), and the plump one on the *left* that is almost ready to depart for its Arctic breeding grounds (and is in more advanced, brighter breeding plumage). Red knots can double their weight in two weeks during the stopover in Delaware Bay.

This is the wing of a red knot caught during fall migration on the Atlantic coast of Argentina in December. It is midway through its main flight-feather (or primary) molt. There are ten primaries, and the three outermost ones were grown the previous year and are showing signs of wear. The inner five have been recently molted and are new. One feather in between is still growing, and another has only just started to grow and is hidden from view.

Stretching, a red knot shows off its full complement of newly molted flight feathers.

Body molt is routinely examined in red knots captured on Delaware Bay. Most have already changed into reddish breeding plumage by the time they arrive; but to improve their chances of mating, it pays to continue molting so that they arrive on the breeding grounds in tip-top condition. Body feathers are dense because they are primarily used to insulate the birds from cold temperatures.

Molt and Plumage

Vital to the well-being of any bird is the good condition of its feathers, which are essential for flight and insulation. But these delicate structures need to be constantly maintained by preening and regularly replaced by molting. Body plumage is replaced quite frequently, and this sometimes results in a color change. For example, red knots are gray in winter, but by the time they reach Delaware Bay in May their plumage is transformed into rusty red for the breeding season. They stay red for only a few months and molt back to gray in August–September. Replacement of flight feathers takes place only once each year, in fall and winter. It is physically demanding, partly because of the resources needed for growth and partly because lack of a full complement of flight feathers reduces flying efficiency. This makes the birds more vulnerable to predators, such as peregrine falcons. The places where shorebirds molt their flight feathers are as important as any locales in their lives. Long- and short-distance red knots molt differently—the former on their wintering areas in South America, the latter while en route to, or on, their wintering areas. Molting on wintering sites may be better because weather, food, and safety may be more predictable. Molting at stopovers en route to wintering sites may be more risky because of the concentration of avian predators that are also migrating. Red knots that molt during their southbound migration stop over in a few key places, such as the Manomoy National Wildlife Refuge on Massachusetts's Cape Cod and the North Brigantine Natural Area along the southern Atlantic Coast of New Jersey. There they stay for up to ninety days, enough time to completely molt and regrow their flight feathers, before moving south to their wintering areas.

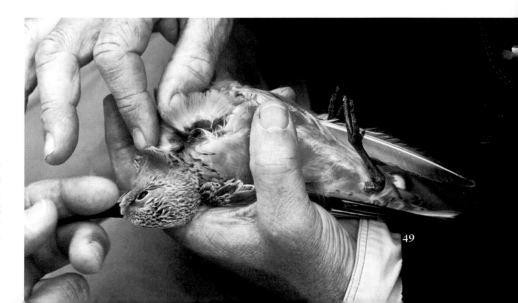

When red knots reach the Arctic, 70 percent of their breeding areas are snow covered, and the birds must forage in icy wetlands. Because available food supplies are so low when they arrive, the birds must rely on the fat resources they brought with them from Delaware Bay.

Red knots and Hudsonian godwits feeding on an intertidal flat in South American wintering areas. Shorebirds usually move in and out with the tide searching for bivalves that are exposed by the changing tides.

While they spend the northern winter in South America, red knots show no evidence of their characteristic red breeding plumage. But during their northward flight, they replace their dull winter plumage with their russet breeding dress. Notice the mix of plumages in this mixed flock of red knots and sanderlings skimming along an Atlantic Ocean beach in Patagonia.

By the time they reach Delaware Bay, nearly all birds are in full breeding plumage.

51

A red knot preens while resting on Delaware Bay.

Plumage varies among individuals, with some more vivid than others, as these two foraging birds illustrate.

One red knot flies with its legs tucked, showing off a perfect set of wing primaries.

A large flock of red knots, dunlins, and short-billed dowitchers fly in front of a sand-and-sod bank beach near Reeds Beach, New Jersey.

During the last days of May, shorebirds on the bay eat frantically to reach optimum weight (*below*). Those that are successful, such as these seven birds in flight (*left*), will reach the Arctic fit enough to breed.

Red knots breed in the Canadian Arctic tundra but sometimes it seems they can't wait. It is not unusual to see them courting and to hear their courtship songs in Delaware Bay (*right*). Females lay four eggs at the end of June, and incubation is shared by both sexes. The breeding plumage of an incubating knot blends perfectly with the subdued colors of the tundra (*below*).

Males do most of the brood rearing; in fact, the females leave and migrate south in mid-July when the chicks are only a few days old (*left*). Born precocial—or relatively mature and mobile—the chicks follow their father within a few days of hatching (*below*). The males depart the breeding grounds before mid-August and the young follow shortly after, finding their way to their winter quarters without any adult assistance.

5 RUDDY TURNSTONES

Ruddy turnstones are the real characters of the Delaware Bay beaches. They are famously omnivorous and adaptable. They are found worldwide, breeding all the way around the Arctic, as far north as there is land; in winter they are found on all the temperate and tropical coasts of the world, from the United States to Argentina, from Britain to Cape Town, and from China to New Zealand. Banding results show that the turnstones that pass through Delaware Bay in May breed in the low Canadian Arctic and winter on the coasts of the southeastern United States, throughout the Caribbean and Gulf of Mexico, and on the northern and eastern coasts of South America to southern Brazil.

Stories abound of turnstone antics and their cosmopolitan diet. On natural shorelines they habitually turn over stones and seaweed in search of insects, mollusks, and other invertebrates, but they will exploit virtually any opportunity that comes their way. For example, they have even been known to feed on a human corpse. For six years, one famous couple of clever turnstones known as Freddy and Freda took the 8:15 A.M. ferry across the three-mile Fal estuary in southwestern England to their foraging areas, returning on the 5:15 P.M. ferry to their roost. However, recent studies show that turnstones annually fly up to 4,750 miles nonstop during migration.

The number of ruddy turnstones stopping over in Delaware Bay in May declined from around 100,000 in 1998 to 15,000 in 2010. There are few systematic counts of turnstones during winter in the West Atlantic Flyway, but the surveys that do exist conflict. Surveys of small sections of Bermuda, Florida, and Texas indicate stable numbers since 1998. However, in the main wintering area in northern Brazil, turnstone numbers have dramatically declined.

Departure weights of ruddy turnstones have also declined, though not to the same extent as red knots. There are various differences between turnstones and knots that may explain why knots have suffered more than turnstones from the depleted food supply. One is that, with their short stubby bills, turnstones are capable of digging pits to gain better access to buried eggs. Though slightly smaller than knots, turnstones also are characteristically more aggressive and better at defending the food they have found. Yet another is that knots mostly arrive in Delaware Bay after long flights with reduced-sized digestive systems and are more reliant on the easily digested eggs than the turnstones, which make shorter flights up the coast from the Caribbean and have a famously diverse diet.

Though ruddy turnstones occur widely along the coasts of the Americas, it is unusual to see more than a few in any particular place. Only on Delaware Bay do they gather in large groups, sometimes in flocks of as many as 1,000, although twenty years ago flocks of 10,000 or more could sometimes be seen. *Below*, a ruddy turnstone (at top) and a red knot join a flock in which both species are roosting together.

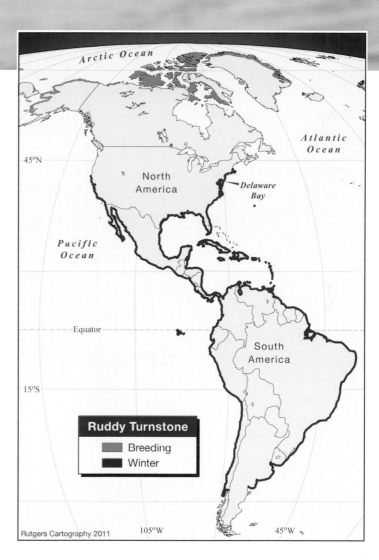

Unlike other shorebirds, male and female ruddy turnstones are quite different. *Above*, the female on the right has more brown than the two males, which have white heads and chestnut in their wings.

Distribution map for ruddy turnstones showing breeding and wintering areas. Little is known about their overall population size.

In the hand, a male ruddy turnstone's striking black-and-white head contrasts with the drab head of a female (*left*). In the fall, juveniles like these two (*right*) are paler than the adults and have light edges to their back feathers, which gives them a scaly appearance.

Turnstones will often forage on beaches while breeding (*above, center*), migrating, and on their wintering grounds (*above, left*) by turning over stones and seaweed to find food. They will also opportunistically feed on almost anything edible, from dead fish to restaurant scraps, and have even been seen feeding on a human corpse. Their ability to turn things over gives them a great advantage in Delaware Bay, especially when horseshoe crab eggs are sparse, because they are able to dig down to gain access to the buried egg masses (*above, right*). Other shorebirds seem incapable of digging, so they gather around the turnstones' pits waiting for an opportunity to steal some eggs.

Aggressive to one another as well as other species, including much bigger ones, ruddy turnstones lunge, peck, and chase to defend food or steal food.

Aggressive Beaks: Turnstones Dig Deep

Ruddy turnstones have short, stout, conical beaks which they normally use to turn over pebbles and seaweed along the shore in search of mollusks and crustaceans, or to probe the nooks and crannies of the Arctic tundra for insects. But in Delaware Bay, when crab eggs become scarce, turnstones dig for eggs—up to six inches beneath the surface of the beach sand, where horseshoe crabs actually lay their egg masses. This has proved to be a fortunate behavioral characteristic for turnstones, since it enables them to feed successfully when egg densities are much lower than those needed by red knots and other shorebirds. But the turnstones' excavations have also proved helpful to the other birds, which soon learn to dart into the pits and steal any uncovered eggs even while they are still being defended by the turnstones. As soon as a turnstone leaves, the other species crowd in to feast on the leftovers. While most shorebirds defend their foraging sites, turnstones are particularly aggressive when defending their pits against other turnstones and shorebirds and even against much larger species, such as laughing gulls, though they draw the line at the bigger herring and great black-backed gulls.

Like red knots, ruddy turnstones can lay down fat resources very quickly by feeding on horseshoe crab eggs in Delaware Bay. They arrive weighing less than 4 ounces and leave at over 6 ounces.

Turnstones often take advantage of human artifacts for roosting and seem to be less fearful of humans than other shorebirds. Clearly they have figured out that this owl (*below*) is only a plastic model. They will roost on fences, docks, and rock piles, as well as on typical shorebird roosting sites on beaches or marshes. Sometimes a thousand or more will roost on a jetty (*top*, *right*), such as this backyard dock on Money Island, New Jersey.

All shorebirds spend considerable time preening their feathers. In this way they clean them and spread oil from the uropygial gland, at the base of their tail, over themselves to ensure that they are waterproof and provide good insulation from cold and wind. Unfortunately, by preening feathers that have become contaminated with fuel oil, shorebirds can also poison themselves.

Epidemiological Mystery

Since 1985, researchers from the Saint Jude Children's Research Hospital and the University of Georgia have been studying avian influenza viruses (AIVs) in red knots, ruddy turnstones, sanderlings, dunlins, short-billed dowitchers, semipalmated sandpipers, and in three gull species: greater black-backed, herring, and laughing gulls. Most of these species come to the bay complete with antibodies of various strains of avian flu, indicating a previous exposure. Only ruddy turnstones arrive on the bay almost free of avian flu antibodies. But within weeks they suffer the equivalent of a flu epidemic that has left researchers puzzled for years. The flu they endure is not the dreaded H5N1 strain known to be dangerous to people, but a common variety of flu not unlike what we experience every year. The birds show no adverse impacts and there is no sign of increased mortality. Researchers combed the region for clues to the mystery, checking roosting sites that turnstones share with other species, or areas where birds were found in particularly dense numbers. One theory is that turnstones may be particularly vulnerable to avian flu in Delaware Bay because it is the only place where turnstones gather in significant numbers. Throughout their range, turnstones usually occur in small densities, often spreading out along long stretches of beach in ones and twos. Because they spend so much time alone, their immune systems may have less exposure—and therefore little chance to develop antibodies to the flu—than other species that overwinter or migrate in large flocks. Delaware Bay may play a role in the ecology of AIVs and how they are transmitted to, and between, shorebird or gull populations. For now, researchers are focusing efforts on understanding how ruddy turnstone ecology interacts with the bay's environment to cause this annual spike in AIV infection in this single species and not in others.

Josh Parris from the Southeast Cooperative Wildlife Disease Study group takes a cloacal swab from a ruddy turnstone to test for avian influenza.

Roosting birds often stretch their wings like this. This male ruddy turnstone shows off his smart black, white, and chestnut plumage that makes him easy to distinguish from other shorebirds in flight (*opposite*).

Shorebirds often concentrate near outflowing creeks, such as the this one in New Jersey between Cooks and Kimbles beaches (*opposite*; the Reeds Beach community is beyond). These creek mouths offer sheltered conditions that favor horseshoe crab spawning. As a result they often have a superabundance of eggs, making them especially attractive as foraging sites for shorebirds.

Above, a ruddy turnstone chases an intruder away from a hole it has dug to reach horseshoe crab egg masses. While such antagonistic behavior is common during feeding, it is much less frequent when birds gather in roosting flocks. They form flocks when they are foraging or roosting, partly to benefit from cooperative vigilance for predators (*opposite*).

68

As the tides rises, water covers the foraging areas, and shorebirds seek places to roost until the tide falls again. Sometimes even the roost sites flood and the birds are forced onto higher ground.

Ruddy turnstones nest throughout the Arctic, often on dry tundra with mosses and lichens. Like many shorebirds, turnstones lay four eggs that hatch at the same time. While incubating, shorebirds shift the eggs so that their narrow ends point inward, making it possible to incubate the whole clutch together. The chicks in the eggs are piping or chipping away at the shell and will likely hatch in a day or two.

6 SANDERLINGS

Stroll along the beaches of the Atlantic Coast, in the heat of August or frigid winds of December, and you'll likely encounter sanderlings, one of our most familiar "sandpipers." But in one respect it is a very odd sandpiper: unlike all other sandpipers it does not have a hind toe. That may seem unimportant, but it is an adaptation for running on sandy beaches, and that—above all else—is what sanderlings do. One can go dizzy watching them feed, running fast behind a retreating ocean wave right to the crest of the next incoming breaker, and back again.

Of the shorebirds that use Delaware Bay as a spring stopover, the sanderling seems less dependent on horseshoe crab eggs. Numbers have fluctuated widely but have been lower in recent years. Nevertheless, the fact that 5 to 10 percent of the entire New World sanderling population stops in Delaware Bay each May shows that it is a very important site for the species.

Even in early May, well before there has been significant horseshoe crab spawning, many thousands of sanderlings can often be seen feeding on small crustaceans and shellfish on the sand flats in the lower part of the bay near Cape May and the nearby Atlantic Coast. But as soon as crab eggs become available, sanderlings pile onto the New Jersey bay beaches in large numbers, though surprisingly few cross to the Delaware side of the bay.

Like ruddy turnstones, sanderlings winter in small groups over a large range—from coastal Massachusetts to the southern tip of South America. Banding studies show that sanderlings that pass through Delaware Bay in May spend the winter in the southeastern United States from Virginia to Florida, on Caribbean islands, and along the north and east coasts of South America as far south as Patagonia. So for some, the northward migration to the Arctic breeding area each spring is a short trip, for others it is as long as that undertaken by red knots. There are pros and cons for short and long migrations: long flights are more risky and require more energy resources, but it may pay to go a long way south for the winter if the destination has more food and there are fewer parasites and pathogens or predators. Those making a short flight to their wintering grounds can lay down energy resources for their return spring migration by eating hard-shelled clams and mole crabs, which take more time to digest and more metabolic energy to turn into fat. For these birds, fat-rich horseshoe crab eggs are a "bonus" food,

Among the gray winter feathers of this sanderling, newly arrived in Delaware Bay, are traces of rusty breeding plumage (*below*). Typically, sanderlings come to Delaware Bay with some breeding plumage. While on the bay, sanderlings continue molting into breeding dress; by the time they leave, most are a rich chestnut brown (*above*).

Like most shorebirds that stop in Delaware Bay, sanderlings breed in the Canadian Arctic. But in winter they range more widely than almost all other shorebirds in the Western Hemisphere, from Cape Cod to the southernmost tip of South America.

A sanderling in the midst of replacing its grayish winter plumage with chestnut brown breeding feathers.

so they are less vulnerable to horseshoe crab population declines. The sanderlings that migrate a longer distance are not so lucky. As with red knots, these sanderlings are more reliant on horseshoe crab eggs because they migrate long distances and have a much shorter period to recover lost body reserves and build up the fat they need to get to the Arctic on time to breed.

Thus, two rather different groups of sanderlings stop over in Delaware Bay, which is one of the few sites in the Western Hemisphere where large numbers of sanderlings gather. This mix of short- and long-distance migrant sanderlings may be one reason for the dramatically different sanderling plumages seen on the bay: some have the full russet plumage of breeders while others are still in their gray winter plumage.

Stopover numbers of sanderlings in Delaware Bay have not declined in the same way as red knots, semipalmated sandpipers, and ruddy turnstones. But they now arrive and depart the bay at a lower weight than they did before the peak harvest of crabs in the mid-1990s. Could the collapse of horseshoe crab eggs have caused a shift in which group feeds on crabs' eggs? Are short-distance migrants taking other food, leaving only long-distance migrants scrambling for fewer horseshoe crab eggs? This may explain the lower arrival and departure weights.

Much of our understanding of sanderlings comes from a patchwork of studies. Generally, this species is not well understood because in winter its population is distributed in small numbers over thousands of miles of sandy beach. Like other shorebirds, sanderlings have suffered from the loss of coastal habitats to development and human disturbance. Sanderlings are highly faithful to their wintering and stopover sites, so disturbance can cause them to abandon good feeding areas or safe roosts for less optimal sites. Oil spills are a significant threat to sanderlings because they spend so much time in the ocean surf and can easily become oiled, even in a light spill. Sanderlings are also at risk when feeding on beaches. Smaller than other shorebirds, they often feed with large gulls at the water's edge. It is not uncommon to see an unwary sanderling end up an easy meal for an alert great black-backed gull that had been feeding on overturned horseshoe crabs.

Oil Spills

Oil spills that taint the Delaware Bay and Atlantic Coast beaches can have major effects on shorebird feeding, preening, and weight gain. In turn, this can affect their ability to migrate, breed, or survive. Observations following the 1996 *Anitra* oil spill on New Jersey's Atlantic Coast indicated that half the sanderlings and semipalmated plovers feeding on oiled beaches were initially disturbed by clean-up crews. People walking, swimming, or sunbathing disturbs only 2 to 3 percent of the shorebirds feeding along the tide line. Clean-up crews were present for two to three weeks, and this disturbance can have major impacts on the availability and suitability of foraging sites. Before the clean-up crews arrived each morning, these two species, the only ones studied, spent significantly more time preening, and less time feeding, than shorebirds that were not oiled. They not only ingested the oil, but they spread it over more of their bodies, increasing potential thermal stress because the feathers were no longer waterproof or provided protection from cold and wind. Some people may argue that these effects do not impact long-term behavior or survival. However, laboratory observations were also made of sanderlings that had small amounts of oil from the *Anitra* spill applied to their breast feathers while an equal number of sanderlings were swabbed with water. Those with oil spent more time preening and less time foraging and resting than birds that were not oiled, and over a one-month period the oiled birds lost weight while the control birds maintained their weight. The loss of weight for migrants that stop over on bay or ocean beaches to gain weight could cause initial mortality, failure to migrate or breed, and reduced long-term survival.

Sanderlings captured on Delaware Bay with cannon nets and fitted with U.S. Fish and Wildlife Service metal bands (*above*) and inscribed leg flags for future identification. They are also weighed (*right*) and measured to determine their condition. Multiple catches through the stopover season enable scientists to monitor the birds' progress in laying down the resources of fat and protein they need to fly to the Arctic and breed successfully.

Left, two sanderlings: the bird on the left is covered with a light coat of oil. Birds will preen their feathers to remove the oil, ingesting it and suffering nonlethal but damaging effects, which are worsened if the bird is repeatedly oiled. This is often the case in oil spills because most shorebirds feed at the water's edge. (Photo by Glen Tepke)

Right, sanderlings forage for horseshoe crab eggs on a Delaware Bay beach at low tide.

After arriving from their southern wintering areas, sanderlings feed on horseshoe crab eggs on Delaware Bay (*above*). But they also move back and forth several times a day to forage on Atlantic Coast beaches for small clams and mole crabs (*below*).

Most of the year, sanderlings forage along sandy ocean shores on invertebrates, such as clams, mussels, and mole crabs (*far right*). Only in Delaware Bay do they feed on horseshoe crab eggs (*near right*). Delaware Bay is one of the world's most important sites for sanderlings: every year up to 10 percent of the Western Hemisphere's total sanderling population passes through the bay.

Below, sanderlings, short-billed dowitchers, and a dunlin discover a clump of horseshoe crab eggs on a Delaware Bay beach while a red knot approaches to see what they've found.

Two sanderlings probe for buried horseshoe crabs eggs on a bay beach.

What Makes a Good Roost?

Shorebirds need to roost during every high tide, every day. While migrating, most feed for as long as they can, but at nightfall or when the tide covers foraging areas, they gather in flocks to rest, digest food, and preen. Species differ: sanderlings roost and feed throughout the day, stopping only during high tide, while oystercatchers may roost for all but three or four hours when the mussel beds are exposed at low tide. On Delaware Bay, red knots roost almost every night on the Atlantic Coast and fly back and forth each day to the bay beaches to feed. What makes a good roost site? The beaches and marshes surrounding Hereford Inlet and Stone Harbor Point exemplify the desirable qualities. First, higher ground remains available no matter how high the tide rises. This is very important during the highest spring tides. Second, the marsh islands and the long sand peninsula of Stone Harbor Point create protection for roosting shorebirds from ground predators such as foxes and house cats. The marsh islands are surrounded by deep tidal streams, and the peninsula provides a clear line-of-sight in every direction for as far as one can see. Sleeping shorebirds will know something is approaching long before it reaches them. The third ideal factor is nearby food sources.

This combination of high ground, protection from predators, and proximity to good foraging varies among different roost sites on Delaware Bay. In New Jersey, the roost at Hereford Inlet does not provide easy access to food. The roost at the state's Heislerville impoundment, where thousands of shorebirds roost each day in May, is not subject to tides and is only a short flight from marsh feeding areas important for semipalmated sandpipers, short-billed dowitchers, and dunlins. Egg Island Point is both close to food and safe from ground predators but does not always have higher ground available during spring tides. In Delaware, Mispillion Harbor, another important roost on the bay, has good access to food but is not safe from predators.

Wind on a beach becomes dangerous because of blowing sand. *Above,* a group of sanderlings on a beach in New Jersey attempts to roost in a howling wind that would sandblast paint off a house or car. Often shorebirds will seek shelter in small depressions in the sand or behind wrack or clumps of vegetation. They might also move to a more sheltered roost site.

Left, stretching its wing, a sanderling shows off a new set of wing primaries.

A flock of sanderlings sleeps at an evening roost, *below.* In roosting, flocks birds frequently open an eye to look out for predators; in this way there are always a few birds keeping watch.

Opposite, sanderlings are much smaller than red knots (seen in the background) and ruddy turnstones but larger than semipalmated sandpipers and many other sandpipers. Their small size means that they often lose out to knots, turnstones, and gulls when foraging for horseshoe crab eggs.

Most shorebirds feed at the high tide line where the bay's light surf frees eggs buried in sand. When egg numbers are low or there are too many competing birds, sanderlings often work together in small groups to dig down into depressions that mark where horseshoe crabs have buried their eggs (*above*). When their stomachs are full, sanderlings rest or preen while they digest their meals (*right*).

Shorebirds not only need to feed but also to sleep and to preen their feathers; disturbances, whether by humans or predators, interrupt these critically important activities.

Foraging for horseshoe crab eggs along the bay shoreline, sanderlings run in and out with each wave, eating stranded eggs (*opposite*). Later they roost in tightly packed flocks (*below*).

Like nearly all the shorebirds that come to Delaware Bay in May, sanderlings nest in the Canadian Arctic. They are often found in dry tundra near lakes or rivers, where they forage. Their chestnut brown color makes them virtually undetectable to predators (*below*). Like most Arctic-nesting shorebirds, sanderlings lay four eggs (*right*). Their chicks are precocial, and are able to forage for themselves soon after they hatch (*opposite*).

7 MUD BIRDS

Beyond the beaches and horseshoe crabs that make Delaware Bay so special for migratory shorebirds lies a vast expanse of salt marsh and mud flats that are important in their own right for other groups of shorebirds. Each spring hundreds of thousands of northbound semipalmated sandpipers, least sandpipers, short-billed dowitchers, and dunlins fly into the salt marsh and mudflats looking for marine worms, mollusks, bivalves, and horseshoe crab eggs. They are often unseen, tucked away among the stems of *spartina* grass or along the shores of several hundred miles of tidal rivers. You can often see them in the distance: flocks ascending from a vast green blanket of spartina, fluidly acting as a single entity flying off elsewhere to set down and probe the mud.

Like red knots and ruddy turnstones, these shorebirds nest in the high Arctic and are also severely constrained for time during their spring migrations. They need to make it to their Arctic nesting grounds in time to take advantage of the abundant resources of the short Arctic summer. But, as with red knots, getting there on time can be difficult. Although the mud birds rely on invertebrates throughout the year, research conducted during the 1980s found that horseshoe crab eggs comprised at least half their diet. In the past, when horseshoe crabs occurred in abundance, they spawned on sandy bars within tidal creeks and even along sod banks. Many of these eggs became available to shorebirds through normal tidal flow; birds fed on them as well as on the invertebrates of the mudflats. But as crab numbers fell, most crab breeding stopped in the marsh. That left the many species that were feeding in the marshes and mudflats in the same compromised situation as the beach-feeding red knots and ruddy turnstones. Semipalmated sandpipers, most strikingly, have shown a decline in their condition similar to that experienced by red knots.

Obviously, in the absence of abundant horseshoe crab eggs, the salt marsh's natural productivity becomes even more important for various mud bird species—both in the spring and autumn. The late summer/fall southbound flight is less demanding because of a less urgent time schedule and the autumnal abundance of marine worms, crustaceans, and bivalves. All three peep sandpipers (semipalmated, western, and least), dunlins, and dowitchers, as well as black-bellied plovers, whimbrel, and many other shorebird species, come to the bay and the nearby Atlantic

A group of semipalmated sandpipers (*left*) searches for crab eggs amid spawning horseshoe crabs. Semipalmated sandpipers typically devour crab eggs in marshes, along creek edges, and on sandy mudflats.

Semipalmated sandpipers (*right, in foreground*) are tiny compared to othershorebirds, like the dunlin in the background.

Coast marshes to restore themselves before moving on to their many different wintering areas. Some, like semipalmated sandpipers, migrate to South America's northern coast. Others, such as the dunlins, fan out through every productive marsh from New Jersey to the southeastern United States and beyond.

After the mudbirds vacate the Delaware Bay and Atlantic Coast marshes each fall for the southeastern United States and equatorial regions of the Western Hemisphere, they face a variety of threats. These include mangrove swamps converted to shrimp and rice farms, subsistence hunting, an increasing prevalence of diseases and parasites, and oil and chemical spills. But for thousands of years these birds have persisted in returning each spring to Delaware Bay. It is their refuge and—provided we remain careful and vigilant—the bay's mudflats and marshes will remain a life-sustaining, critical link in the annual cycle of their wondrous migrations.

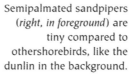

Standing in front of two semipalmated sandpipers, a least sandpiper is easily recognized by its smaller size and yellow legs (*left*).

A dunlin in breeding plumage (*below*), with its distinctive black underside and long, drooping bill, usually uses the bay marshes and feeds less frequently on bay beaches. Dunlins occur in equally large numbers in the spring on Delaware Bay and in the fall in the Atlantic Coast marshes.

Short-billed dowitchers (*left*) are commonly found in Delaware Bay marshes. They are easily identified because of their long bill and chestnut-russet coloration. When flying, dowitchers show a conspicuous white patch on their back and have a characteristic "sewing machine" action while probing for prey. While red knots are also chestnut, dowitchers are darker overall, have longer legs and a more slender bill, and appear less chunky.

Semipalmated Sandpipers

Although the semipalmated sandpiper remains the most abundant shore-bird species on Delaware Bay during the May stopover, it has—like other stopover visitors—suffered tremendous declines. Unlike many shorebird species that make both short and long flights to widely spaced wintering areas, nearly all semipalmated sandpipers make a relatively long migration to the same area. Today the numbers are much reduced, probably less than 200,000 birds—another causality of the collapse of the horseshoe crab population on the bay. Semipalmated sandpipers have shown a significant decrease in average weight over the last fifteen years and, as with red knots, a smaller proportion of the population is reaching the weight necessary to reach the Arctic and breed successfully. But this sandpiper

A large flock of semipalmated sandpipers forages amid spawning horseshoe crabs on Slaughter Beach, Delaware (*left*). It is estimated that nearly half of the Western Hemisphere's population comes through Delaware Bay. The semipalmated sandpaper was named for its partially webbed (semipalmated) feet (*bottom left*).

faces other serious problems.

During the birds' fall migration they concentrate by the thousands in the Bay of Fundy in New Brunswick, Canada, a Delaware Bay–sized estuary with a thirty-foot tidal range. From there they make their way to their primary wintering area in French Guiana and Suriname, where declines are also apparent. In 2009, scientists from the New Jersey Audubon Society led an expedition to these wintering grounds. An aerial survey uncovered a dramatic 90 percent decline in the wintering population compared to counts done during the 1980s. They also found evidence of widespread hunting of the sandpipers for food, especially in Suriname. The losses in these wintering areas are hard to estimate, but they can only exacerbate the losses associated with Delaware Bay. A new program developed by New Jersey Audubon provides money for gas and other supplies for conservation officers to assist them in their efforts to enforce hunting bans.

Above, birds are fitted with yellow flags by Mizrahi's group on their Suriname wintering grounds, and some of these birds are seen each year in Delaware Bay.

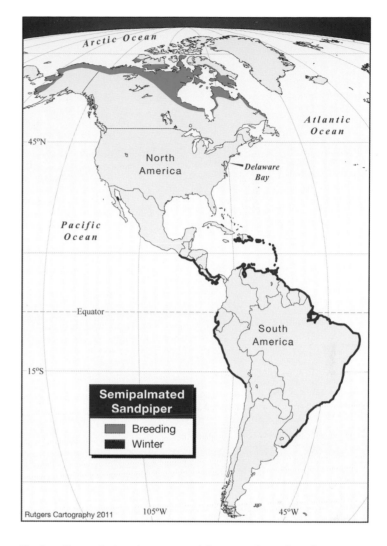

The breeding and wintering ranges of the semipalmated sandpiper. Unlike most Delaware Bay shorebirds that range widely in winter, this sandpiper winters in a relatively small area centered on French Guiana, Suriname, and northern Brazil.

One of the bay's major research projects focuses on the survival of semipalmated sandpipers. David Mizrahi (*above, center, photo by Kevin T. Karlson*) of the New Jersey Audubon Society, the research project leader, and his team extract sandpipers from mist nets at a Heislerville, New Jersey, impoundment so that biologists can band and determine their condition (*top*).

Left, a semipalmated sandpiper incubates its eggs in the Arctic. This is one of the few shorebird species whose world population is confined to the Western Hemisphere that passes through Delaware Bay.

Management of Impoundments for Shorebirds

All shorebirds need habitat to find food and to roost safely while they digest, rest, or sleep. On Delaware Bay, food is determined by the number of horseshoe crabs laying eggs. Roosting sites are more restricted because birds need very specific habitat with good sightlines to reduce the threats of predators. These roosts also must be high enough to stay out of the water even at the highest tides, and the closer to food the better. There are only a limited number of places on the bay that fit this description, so managers are increasingly looking at waterfowl impoundments as potential new roost habitats. These impoundments were an important new innovation for protecting waterfowl fifty years ago. Hundreds were created all along the Atlantic Coast to help restore waterfowl numbers. There are waterfowl impoundments on both sides of Delaware Bay, including the Heislerville Wildlife Management Area in New Jersey and, in Delaware, the Ted Harvey Conservation Area, Little Creek Wildlife Area, and the Prime Hook and Bombay Hook national wildlife refuges.

In 2005 wildlife managers with the New Jersey Division of Fish and Wildlife experimented with water levels by trying to keep only inches of water over the entire forty-acre Heislerville impoundment. The impoundment's natural topography provided perfect roosting habitat, and in just a few seasons more than 40,000 shorebirds—mostly semipalmated sandpipers and dunlins—were using the impoundment. They were nearly all using it for roosting at high tide, when foraging areas are flooded. Delaware biologists are planning to alter management of all their impoundments to account for shorebird roosting habitat during the spring and fall and for waterfowl at other times.

Willets (*above*) breed commonly in the salt marshes of Delaware Bay and the nearby Atlantic Coast. They nest on the ground, pulling marsh grasses over the nest to hide it from predators. They will burst from their nest when disturbed and can be very noisy, calling *pill-will-willet* almost incessantly. They nest in loose colonies, which provide some mutual protection from predators.

A tightly packed, mixed flock of semipalmated sandpipers, semipalmated plovers, dunlins, and dowitchers, with black skimmers flying overhead, at Heislerville, New Jersey. During high tide, this saltwater impoundment hosts flocks of thousands of shorebirds. Although most go there to roost, some are able to exploit the area's invertebrate food resources. Managers control water levels so that they range from zero to a few inches, allowing a vast foraging area for short-legged shorebirds.

A flock of dowitchers, with a few semipalmated sandpipers, forages on the mudflat (*above*). By foraging in mixed-species flocks, shorebirds reduce competition for prey such as horseshoe crab eggs or invertebrates because each species tends to feed in a slightly different way.

Black-bellied plovers feed on sandy beaches, mudflats, and in shallow water (*left*). Although they are one of the least common species in Delaware Bay, these plovers are widespread in the Atlantic coastal marshes of New Jersey. Among the shorebirds of Delaware Bay, its jet black breast and silvery upper parts make it easy to identify (*above*).

93

Three views of semipalmated sandpipers: alert and flying with sanderlings on Cooks Beach, New Jersey, with Pierces Point in the background (*below*); feeding on marsh invertebrates on a mudflat near Greenwich, New Jersey (*opposite, top*); and searching a bay beach, along with ruddy turnstones, for horseshoe crab eggs (*opposite, bottom*).

A semipalmated sandpiper consumes a single horseshoe crab egg (*left*); semipalmated sandpipers feed among breeding horseshoe crabs, including some overturned by the light surf (*right*); two birds contest each other's right to use a portion of beach about the size of

Two semipalmated plovers battle to control a small area of mud flat at the Heislerville impoundment (*above*). Thousands of these plovers use the impoundment to both feed and roost when high tides cover most foraging habitat. These brief battles between shorebirds during migration are much less heated than territorial disputes between breeding birds, such as these two American oystercatchers, which breed on both the bay and ocean beaches during the shorebird stopover (*right*).

A flock of dunlins accompanied by one sanderling (center, with white underside) alight on a bay beach to feed amid breeding horseshoe crabs. The dunlin is one of the least studied shorebirds on the bay and little is known of its population status.

98

A pair of aptly named black-necked stilts remains on a beach being vacated by semipalmated sandpipers. Although common on the Pacific and Gulf coasts, black-necked stilts rarely breed on Delaware Bay. However, they do regularly breed on the Delaware side of the bay, including at Bombay Hook National Wildlife Refuge. Stilts winter in the southeastern United States and South America.

A flock of dunlins, semipalmated sandpipers, and red knots flies after being disturbed from a creek mouth near Cooks Beach, New Jersey (*above*). Dunlins (*right*) are easily identified by the dark patch on their bellies and their relatively large and down-curved bills.

A short-billed dowitcher searches a bay beach for horseshoe crab eggs (*right*). Dowitchers normally probe for marine worms and other invertebrates with a characteristic "sewing machine" motion. In flight, dowitchers are often mistaken for red knots but can be distinguished by their longer bills (*above*).

8 GULLS

A sea of white birds mills along the shore at Moores Beach. Some squabble over tiny green horseshoe crab eggs floating in the waves, others peck furiously at the tide edge, and still others probe for buried eggs higher on the wet sand. Bent over, a few devour the insides of upturned female horseshoe crabs that failed to return to the bay when the tides fell. Some gulls rest in tight groups higher on the beach, some engage in courtship wherever they can carve out a small, undisturbed space. But most are intent on feeding. All along Delaware Bay, the tideline and beach are literally covered with gulls feeding rapidly to build up fat reserves for breeding. In some places the gulls outnumber the shorebirds, while elsewhere scattered gulls feed within dense shorebird flocks.

Besides serving as a stopover for shorebirds, Delaware Bay hosts a large influx of gulls in May and June. They are present at other times of the year, but their numbers decline dramatically when the horseshoe crab eggs disappear. Three species of gulls feed or roost along the bayshore in early spring: herring gulls, great black-backed gulls, and laughing gulls. In the early 1900s, only laughing gulls bred in New Jersey. But with the advent of large open landfills that provided food for gulls during the winter, herring gulls and black-backed gulls moved south from their northern breeding ranges and invaded New Jersey. The first herring gull bred in New Jersey in 1948 and great black-backs followed shortly afterward. While herring and great black-backed gulls occur in Delaware Bay all year, laughing gulls migrate south for the winter.

Although all three species breed in the Atlantic Coast salt marshes from Barnegat Bay to Cape May, and exploit the annual availability of both horseshoe crabs and horseshoe crab eggs in Delaware Bay, it is the large colony of more than 20,000 pairs of laughing gulls at Ring Island, behind Stone Harbor, New Jersey, that has the biggest impact on consumption of horseshoe crab eggs in nearby Delaware Bay. Herring and black-backed gulls are outnumbered by a ratio of 10 to 1 by laughing gulls and focus their foraging efforts mainly on overturned horseshoe crabs. For laughing gulls, horseshoe crab eggs provide a readily available food source for courtship feeding, for foraging for themselves, and for feeding their growing young.

The competition between shorebirds and gulls for horseshoe crab eggs takes two forms: the gulls can prevent the much smaller shorebirds

from having access to the surf and tide lines where horseshoe eggs are most abundant (spatial competition), and the gulls can actually deplete the horseshoe crab eggs (resource competition). Determining the effect of gull competition with shorebirds is difficult because the numbers of shorebirds and gulls, and horseshoe crabs and egg availability, shift during the day, the season, and with the tides. Shorebirds respond to these factors by shifting locations along the bay, even moving daily from the Jersey to the Delaware side of the bay, or over to the Stone Harbor marshes. The competition between shorebirds and gulls for these limited resources, however, has more dire consequences for the shorebirds than the gulls. That is because the gulls are local residents and have to fly only to nearby breeding colonies, while the shorebirds must lay down enough fat in a short period of time to fly thousands of miles to reach breeding grounds in the Arctic.

Herring and great black-backed gulls can also affect horseshoe crabs themselves as they prey on the spawning populations on the beaches. As much as 10 percent of the spawning horseshoe crabs may be left stranded on the beach because of wave action during spawning (which overturns them) or disorientation during their return to the sea. Stranded horseshoe crabs can withstand the stress from drying for up to twenty-four hours, and often return to the water during the next high tide. However, each spring gulls may kill over a thousand crabs per mile of spawning beaches, which is a high toll on crab populations.

While some people have called for control of gulls to reduce competition with the migrant shorebirds, this solution is problematic for several reasons. Demonstrating that the competition is detrimental to the shorebirds is difficult. It is nearly impossible to keep the gulls from the preferred feeding sites (and many methods have been tried). Finally, laughing gulls are native to New Jersey, and it is important to protect the Jersey laughing gulls because they are such an important part of the U.S. bird population. The only solution is to increase the number of spawning horseshoe crabs, thereby increasing the food resource, and reducing any effect the gulls may have on the ability of shorebirds to gain sufficient weight to migrate long distances.

All three species of gulls that breed in New Jersey and Delaware come to Delaware Bay to feed on horseshoe crabs and eggs. Laughing gulls have a strikingly black head (*top*), great black-backed gulls have a black back (*bottom, left*), and herring gulls have a gray back (*bottom, right*). Herring gulls are about three times heavier than laughing gulls.

While early in May dense flocks of adult laughing gulls forage on the bay beaches (*right*), later in May and June the number of adults decreases because they must incubate eggs they have laid in their Atlantic Coast colonies. Unlike laughing gulls, most herring and great black-backed gulls that forage for horseshoe crab eggs are mainly immatures.

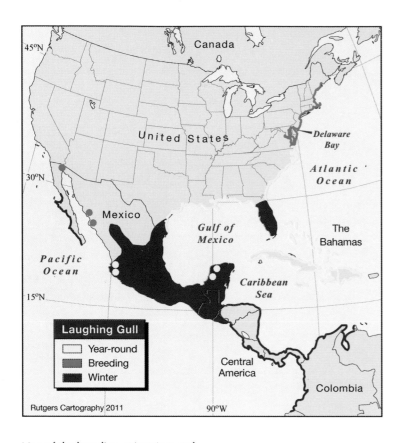

Map of the breeding, migrating, and wintering ranges of laughing gulls. Laughing gulls leave New Jersey in September and October, many flying as far as Mexico's Yucatan Peninsula. In April they return to Delaware Bay and their breeding colonies.

In the 1970s, Joanna Burger began a long-term study of laughing gulls using wing tags to identify individuals. This work showed that nesting gulls will fly thirty to forty-five miles to forage. Shown here (*right*) is a young of the year, able to fly. (Photo by Michael Gochfeld)

Most immature laughing gulls remain on the wintering grounds in the southern United States and the Gulf of Mexico. Only a few return to Delaware Bay to feed on horseshoe crab eggs (*right*).

Laughing gulls will hover over a predator or person, giving long *kek-kek-kek* calls to warn other colony members of impending danger.

New Jersey: The Epicenter for Laughing Gulls

Laughing gulls are truly "Jersey gulls." New Jersey is the center of their breeding range and hosts the highest breeding population. Laughing gulls breed along the Atlantic Coast from Maine to Florida, along the Gulf Coast, and on islands in the Caribbean. Surprisingly, there are far fewer colonies in Delaware; some breed at Rehoboth Bay in Sussex County, but the colony sizes there are small.

From the 1960s to the late 1980s, the U.S. population increased to about 250,000 pairs, due to the presence of garbage dumps; the Jersey population accounted for about 25 percent of the U.S. total breeding population. Then the New Jersey population decreased by a third from the late 1980s to the mid-1990s because of gull control at New York's nearby John F. Kennedy International Airport and competition for nesting sites with the larger gulls. Because the Jersey Shore is invaded by hordes of tourists in the spring and summer and coastal development has reached an all-time high, herring and great black-backed gulls nested on the highest places in salt marshes, forcing the native laughing gulls to move lower on the marshes and making them vulnerable to tidal flooding and storms. Reproductive success declined and some marsh island laughing gull colonies have disappeared.

The number of laughing gulls feeding along the Delaware Bay also declined from the early 1990s to the early 2000s. On Delaware Bay, laughing gulls also face competition from the bigger gulls for foraging places. Although there may be intense competition between laughing gulls and shorebirds for horseshoe crab eggs during spring migration, laughing gulls are an important part of the U.S. avifauna and deserve protection.

In New Jersey and Delaware, laughing gulls nest mainly in salt-marsh grasses, selecting the highest places in the marsh. Sometimes nests can be very close together, as they are on Clam Island in Forsythe National Wildlife Refuge. Young gulls normally remain on their nest, but when they wander into the tall grass they are nearly impossible to find. This young bird (*right*), begging food from its parent, is enclosed in a small pen to make it possible for Burger to study its growth and development. (Photos by J. Burger)

Swamping: Size and Numbers Matter

Competition for horseshoe crab eggs has two components: space and availability of the crab eggs. Generally bigger birds can displace smaller birds in any foraging situation because they can win in a fight. The bigger the size difference, the more likely it is that the smaller birds will forgo even an attempt to displace the bigger birds. Often birds of similar size fight the most because the outcome of a direct attack is unclear—either bird could win. Normally gulls will displace shorebirds from a preferred foraging site along the surf. And the larger herring and great black-backed gulls will displace laughing gulls from foraging sites.

However, density matters. Gulls have a difficult time, and are often reluctant, to wade in among a very dense flock of foraging shorebirds. It is as if the gulls cannot find a place to move among the tight group of shorebirds, and often remain on the edge. Thus, by feeding in dense flocks, shorebirds can retain their preferred foraging sites along the surf. Similarly, a herring gull or a great black-backed gull often will not invade a dense, noisy flock of laughing gulls. The trouble occurs when the foraging shorebirds are disturbed by people, dogs, or boats. Not only do these disturbances force the shorebirds to stop eating and expend energy flying away, but shorebirds also are more wary and take longer to return to the beach. This gives the gulls a chance to infiltrate in large numbers and prevents the shorebirds from returning to their preferred foraging sites, those that offer the highest numbers of available horseshoe crab eggs.

Laughing gulls, such as these near the Reeds Beach jetty, often pack together so tightly when they forage on horseshoe crabs eggs that no other birds can land.

Often people, dogs, or predators will scare away flocks of shorebirds, leaving the gulls to forage undisturbed.

Experiments to decrease the competition between laughing gulls and shorebirds for horseshoe crab eggs involved creating a "gull exclosure" by stringing monofilament lines over foraging areas, as restaurant owners often do at shore restaurants (*left*). The lines were successful in keeping gulls away all the time, but shorebirds would only enter the enclosure when eggs were extremely scarce.

Left, Lawrence Niles removes a laughing gull from a net so that a University of Georgia team (*below*) can test its blood for avian influenza antibodies. These tests determined that the gulls were not a source of the avian influenza found in ruddy turnstones.

While laughing gulls (*above*) normally return to breed in their third year, herring gulls do not breed until they are four or five years old, and great black-backed gulls (*below*) usually wait until they are five or six. It is possible to age gulls before they reach full maturity, although plumage varies considerably. Generally, the darker brown the gull's plumage, the younger the bird.

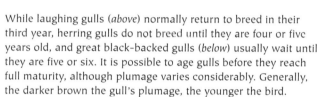

Because horseshoe crab eggs concentrate in coves and creek entrances, gulls flock to these places, often crowding out the smaller shorebirds. People on the Reed's Beach jetty watch the gulls (*opposite*).

Laughing gulls are kleptoparasites, often attacking other gulls to steal their food (*opposite*). *Right and below,* a fortunate laughing gull with a relatively rare find— an intact, unearthed horseshoe crab egg mass, which contains up to 5,000 eggs. It is evident that this bird recently returned to the nesting colony because it has a faint pink tinge on its breast feathers, indicative of a fresh molt and early courtship. The pink tinge fades very quickly and is gone by late May.

Above, a male laughing gull with a fiddler crab in its beak lands next to a prospective female mate (*opposite*). Part of the mating ritual of gulls is for the male to feed the slightly smaller female. This has the advantage of providing the female with more food than she could obtain on her own. In the early stages of courtship this feeding can occur away from the nesting colony, but in a few days the gulls continue this behavior at their nest site.

Following courtship feeding, the female and male call to one another and copulation soon follows. During copulation, the male flaps his wings and the white underwing linings are visible across the marsh. Laughing gulls sometimes copulate up to thirty times a day.

A great black-backed gull feeds
on an overturned horseshoe crab.

Herring gulls, which also feed on overturned crabs, forage on a range of invertebrates they find in the surf (*below*). The red spot on their lower mandible (*right*) directs the attention of their very young chicks to their bill for feeding. The pecking of a young chick on that red spot stimulates the adult to regurgitate food, such as horseshoe crab eggs, pieces of overturned female crabs, or other invertebrates.

9 TIDAL RIVERS AND MARSHES

Riding in a boat along the Delaware bayshore in early spring, it is easy to believe you are alone in the world. The bay waters stretch for miles toward the horizon and the shoreline—mostly protected through public or conservation-group ownership—is fringed with salt marshes, mudflats, sandbars, and tidal rivers. The health of Delaware Bay depends on these tidal habitats, especially the tidal rivers, creeks, and salt marshes that the tides feed and drain twice a day. This estuarine ecosystem is one of the most expansive in the northeastern United States and supports a unique mix of wildlife that reflects its size and location.

The bay is uniquely located—a zone of overlap between the ranges of many northern and southern species. This explains the tremendous diversity of birds and is one reason why New Jersey is the site of the annual World Series of Birding, which the New Jersey Audubon Society sponsors and hosts at the mouth of the bay in Cape May. The bay is also an important wintering area for southbound waterfowl and waterbirds because it is one of the northern-most estuaries that remain ice free throughout the winter.

People also depend on the health of this ecosystem. The tidal marshes provide much-needed shoreline protection from storms and high tides, removal of nutrients and pollutants from farm and city storm water runoff, nursery habitat for fish and shellfish, and wide open space for diverse forms of recreation from kayaking to hunting.

A male marsh wren sings to advertise his territory. Males build several nests to attract a mate, which selects the nest where she will lay her eggs.

A salt marsh at low tide with muddy creeks, a habitat that is packed with a rich invertebrate fauna that supports birds such as rails, herons, and egrets.

Besides the Delaware River, the longest free-flowing river in the eastern United States, many rivers flow into Delaware Bay. The most important are the Maurice, Cohansey, and Salem rivers in New Jersey and the Mispillion, Leipsic, Smyrna, and Christina rivers in Delaware. Each river has its own history, but all were vital for transport of food and timber out of the region, the harvest and processing of fish and shellfish, and ultimately, the development of bay industries including shipbuilding, glass manufacture, petroleum refining, and transport.

Historically, most bayshore residents survived by either farming or fishing the bay. Early in the settlement of the region, bayshore farmers added to their arable lands by "reclaiming" or draining bay and river marshes. In 1695, a surveyor, Thomas Budd, recognized the agricultural potential of the marshes by reporting to his employers that "the mosquito-infested marshes could then be turned into pasture for cattle and meadow as rich as that along the Thames River." Throughout the eighteenth and nineteenth centuries, New Jersey and Delaware farmers built dikes with tide gates and transformed thousands of acres of tidally flooded wetland into salt hay impoundments or agricultural lands. These impounded areas were so productive they commanded a higher price per acre than adjacent upland farms. Most of this reclaimed land was devoted to salt hay, a product valued for its resistance to rot and used for mattresses. But many acres, especially along the rivers, were farmed for crops such as oats, corn, and wheat. Construction and maintenance of dikes required large investments of time and money. This led to the development of meadow bank companies composed of farmers with land in the impounded area. The Greenwich Meadow Bank Corporation on the Cohansey River persists to this day, although its main dike was breached during a 1993 storm.

Today nearly all of the dikes are gone and the diked fields that remain are no longer used for crops. Many find a new use as stopover sites for migratory birds. In the 1960s federal and state biologists started managing impounded water to create habitat for waterfowl resting and feeding. These impoundments, at places such as Bombay Hook National Wildlife Refuge in Delaware and Heislerville Wildlife Management Area in New Jersey, still provide quality habitat for migrant ducks and geese but are also being managed as shorebird stopover habitats. Managed water levels at the Heislerville impoundment provide an ideal high-tide roost for semipalmated sandpipers, dunlin, dowitchers, and other migrants in numbers as high as 40,000 birds.

Captains' houses in Lewes, Delaware (*right*), and Mauricetown, New Jersey (*below*). Both towns were home to thriving commercial fisheries that have long since been depleted. These houses were built on fortunes created from the oyster boom of the late 1800s and early 1900s.

Kayakers enjoy the Maurice River, the largest New Jersey river flowing into Delaware Bay. Commercial traffic on the Maurice supported local industries such as glassmaking, shipbuilding, farming, and fishing.

Instead of dead snags, Delaware Bay ospreys mainly use artificial platforms such as this one constructed on the Maurice River by Citizens United to Protect the Maurice River and Its Tributaries. The platforms are designed to prevent ground predators such as raccoons from eating eggs or chicks. Ospreys are fish eaters.

The Bay's Last Diked Farm

The Burcham farm is the last diked farm on the Maurice River and the Delaware Bay. Begun in 1869, it originally grew vegetables and grains, but through the years the dikes became difficult to maintain from storms and very high tides. The Burcham family established a brick-and-drain tile works on the property, and many of the defective bricks were used to fortify the dikes. The dikes are still intact, mainly to protect the farm and buildings. Most of the marshes along the bay's rivers were diked during the nineteenth and twentieth centuries to control water levels, increase freshwater levels, and allow the planting of crops. Most often the diked areas were used to pasture cattle and to grow hay. Some of the diked marshes along the upper reaches of the rivers, where water was less saline, were planted with corn, oats, and wheat. These dikes were abandoned during the early 1900s because of advances made in agriculture to make uplands more productive and the growing difficulty of maintaining the dikes. Today, only a few diked marshes, such as the Burcham farm, remain.

Breeding Birds of the Salt Marsh

The bay's extensive marshes support a thriving population of coastal plain swamp sparrow, a unique variant of the more common inland swamp sparrow. Not discovered until relatively recently, the stronghold of this rare bird is the midbay region of Delaware Bay. Like Darwin's finches, the coastal plain swamp sparrow has adapted to life in the salt marsh by becoming darker, to better blend into mud flats where they forage, and by having larger bills which they use to catch crustaceans and invertebrates. Their dark grayish color, known as "salt-marsh melanism," distinguishes them from the reddish browns of their inland cousins.

The black rail is the epitome of salt-marsh melanism. This rail uses color and behavior to be Delaware Bay's most secretive and elusive bird. Once ubiquitous in the bay, it has declined dramatically—some estimating that nearly 80 percent of potential breeding areas are now vacant. Making matters worse, the black rail is semicolonial, so the loss of one site could mean the loss of a large number of breeding pairs. Like the coastal plain swamp sparrow, the black rail prefers the high salt marsh that is flooded

Black rails nest in high *Spartina patens* marshes along with coastal plain swamp sparrows, northern harriers, and other rails, including king, sora, clapper, and Virginia rails. Among these rails, the black rail (*above*) is the rarest that nests in Delaware Bay. (Photo by Brian Small)

Willets often utilize high perches to watch for predators. Geolocators are being placed on willets by the New Jersey chapter of the Nature Conservancy to determine migratory pathways and wintering areas.

An oystercatcher incubates its eggs on a bay beach (*below*). Oystercatchers lay three to four eggs in a shallow sandy depression or on salt-marsh wrack deposited by high winter tides. (Photo by Kevin T. Karlson)

Black-necked stilts (*below*) breed in Delaware but not in New Jersey marshes. They generally nest in very loose colonies but depend on group defense to deter predators.

by the tide only a few times each month. This tiny rail spends nearly all of its time under the cover of thick salt-marsh vegetation and uses small mammal tunnels. It rarely sings its "*kick-kee-doo*" song, and then only in the middle of the night.

Not all shorebirds of the bay are Arctic nesters; two species actually nest on the bay. The willet nests throughout the bay in the high marsh or along the marsh-dune interface. It is so abundant that its "*per-will-willet*" call is as pervasive as the sound of wind blowing through the marsh grasses. Delaware Bay has one of the East Coast's highest concentrations of willet. The American oystercatcher nests in the same places but less frequently along the bay, preferring Atlantic Coast beaches and marsh. Oystercatchers probably once fed on oyster beds, long gone because of mechanical harvesting, but now they depend on the bay's abundant mussel beds. The American oystercatcher is designated as a species of conservation concern by most states along the eastern U.S. coastline, and considerable effort is being made to restore its populations to healthy levels. Two other shorebirds, the American avocet and the black-necked stilt, occur rarely on the bay, although stilts have been seen nesting in Bombay Hook National Wildlife Refuge and other sites.

Northern harriers, also called marsh hawks, nest on the ground in the high *Spartina* salt marsh or in reeds at the edge of marshes. (Photo by Kevin T. Karlson)

Snow geese migrate to Delaware Bay and Atlantic coastal marshes by the tens of thousands. They often damage the salt marsh by yanking marsh grass out by the roots, leaving bare mud that accelerates erosion and marsh destruction.

Waterfowl of the Bay

Each winter, Delaware Bay becomes home for tens of thousands of ducks and geese. Long before Canada geese became the scourge of city parks and corporate campuses, Arctic-breeding Canada geese announced the arrival of fall by flying into the bay. Not long after, tens of thousands of greater snow geese arrived to forage on waste grain and graze the fertile pastures and bay marshes. There are now so many geese in the bay that they cover the sky, flying in vast V formations as they move between feeding sites and roost areas in the marsh or sheltered tidal bays. More than 100,000 have been seen at one time in Bombay Hook National Wildlife Refuge alone. During the fall and winter hunting seasons, the air fills with the raucous calls of Canada and snow geese moving about the farms and marshes of the bay.

The bay is well known for its abundant waterfowl. Black ducks nest in the bay's vast marshes, making it one of the most important breeding sites in the eastern United States for this beleaguered bird. During the fall migration, one can find a complete spectrum of waterfowl: ruddy ducks, buffleheads, common goldeneye, northern pintail, green-winged teal, red-breasted mergansers, and greater and lesser scaup. Over 250,000 black and surf scoters have been sighted at the mouth of the bay. This diversity and abundance is possible because the bay itself is a palette of habitats that attracts these species: open bay and bayshore, saline tidal rivers, brackish and freshwater creeks and wooded swamps, vast mud flats and *spartina* marsh, isolated brackish ponds and impounded areas. Some areas are open to hunters each fall; others are far from any human disturbance.

Salt-Marsh Ecology of the Bay

The marsh that fringes the open water of Delaware Bay is one of the most extensive wetlands on the East Coast. Tidal marshes are one of the world's more productive natural habitats, and those on Delaware Bay's marsh are no exception. Marshes have a twice-daily tidal exchange of water that floods thousands of acres of tidal creek, marsh, and mud flat. The Delaware River, one of the nation's last undammed rivers, pours a huge amount of freshwater into the bay every day, decreasing salinity and increasing productivity. The tidal and river flows help cleanse the river of contaminants and decrease the chance of developing oxygen-depleted "dead zones" that plague other estuaries, such as Chesapeake Bay. To a casual observer, the bay's tidal marsh looks all the same, but subtle changes in elevation result in very different vegetation and wildlife. At the low end is marsh that floods every tide and is usually dominated by several forms of *Spartina alterniflora* or salt-marsh cordgrass. Slightly higher marsh is dominated by *Spartina patens*, which only floods on spring tides or tides that occur usually twice a month. Finally, just a few inches higher there is a third zone which floods only on storm tides that periodically force saltwater far inland, killing all but salt-tolerant plants such as *Salicornia*. Most of the bay's marsh breeders, such as northern harriers, willets, clapper rails, and black rails, breed in high marsh.

A Forster's tern gives an alarm call. Nesting in salt marshes, Forster's terns can frequently be seen fishing along the shores of Delaware Bay and resting on docks.

A great egret (*right*) hunts for small fish in a salt marsh. Great egrets nest on islands in the Atlantic coast marshes, as well as in the heron colony on Pea Patch Island in the upper Delaware Bay.

Double-crested cormorants (*left*) gather on an abandoned bulkhead on Bidwell Creek, near Reeds Beach, New Jersey.

A sign welcomes visitors to the Bombay Hook National Wildlife Refuge, one of four national wildlife refuges on the bay. The others are Prime Hook in Delaware, and Cape May and Supawna Meadows in New Jersey.

Types of Delaware Bay marsh. Like all tidal marsh, type depends on elevation relative to high tide. Here there are three types: regularly flooded low marsh dominated by *Spartina alterniflora*; irregularly flooded high marsh dominated by *Spartina patens*; and a third, rarely flooded type that is vegetated with either salicornia or *Iva frutescens*, the common high-tide bush.

Tidal creeks on Delaware Bay (*far left, center*) and tidal mudflats on the bayshore (*far left, bottom*) are home to many wildlife species, including the diamondback terrapin (*left*), the fiddler crab (*below*), and a dense and diverse assemblage of invertebrates that are the primary food for many of the bay's wildlife and fish.

Much of the bayshore is sod bank or eroded marsh devoid of all but the roots of marsh vegetation (*below*). The thin ribbon of sand lying along the high tide line of sod banks (*opposite*) is known as a "wash-over beach." These beaches move inland as the bay erodes the marsh and are usually marginal breeding habitat for horseshoe crabs. This erosion has been occurring since the last ice age, thousands of years ago, but is exacerbated by sea-level rise associated with global climate change.

The schooner *Meerwald*, here sailing past East Point Light at the mouth of the Maurice River, was commissioned in 1928 by the Meerwald family as an oyster boat. In 1942 the U.S. Coast Guard recommissioned the vessel as a fire boat, removing all its masts and adding a diesel engine. After World War II it was used again to dredge oysters and eventually clams, this time under power, until it was retired in the 1980s. The boat was donated to the Schooner Project founded by Megan Wren in 1989 and was designated as New Jersey's official tall ship in 1998. The Delaware Bay Schooner Project became the Bayshore Discovery Project in 2002.

Upriver from where the *Meerwald* docks at Bivalve, the river gradually turns to brackish then fresh water, and is bounded by high bluffs. The upper river supports a much different group of animal and plant species, including bald eagles and wild rice.

The bay salt marsh and tidal creeks (*left*) are the life blood of every organism on Delaware Bay.

The glossy ibis (*below*) often feed on horseshoe crab eggs or newly hatched larvae. Although the bird is not native to New Jersey, it was occasionally sighted here as far back as the 1800s. It underwent a rapid expansion of its breeding range after 1950 and now breeds throughout the East Coast.

128

A flock of ruddy turnstones fly along a bay creek in search of horseshoe crab eggs.

Tidal creeks on Delaware Bay—one in the spring (*top*) and one in the fall (*right*)—support a diverse assemblage of water birds, including great blue herons (*opposite, left*) and clapper rails.

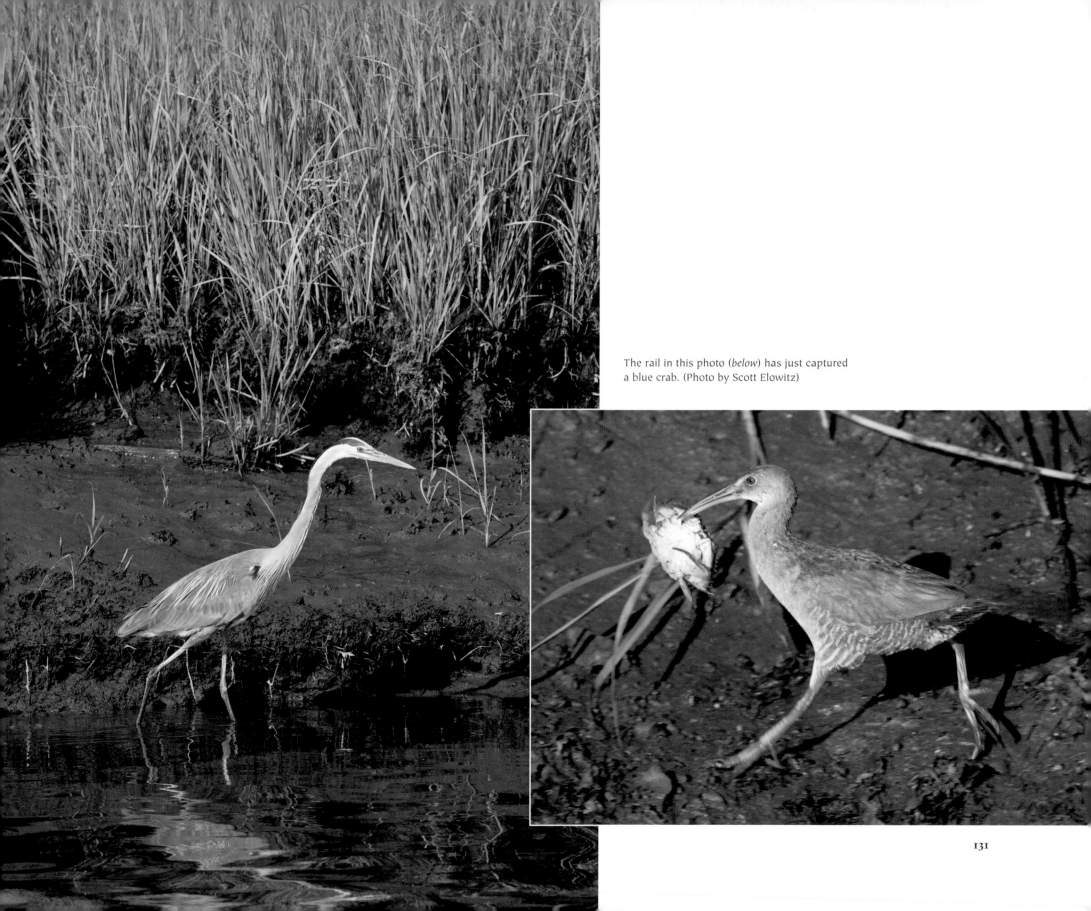

The rail in this photo (*below*) has just captured a blue crab. (Photo by Scott Elowitz)

10 AGAINST THE TIDE
THREATS AND CONSERVATION EFFORTS

In the 1950s the lower Delaware River and Bay comprised one of the most polluted estuaries in the world. In 1973, three years after President Richard Nixon created the U.S. Environmental Protection Agency, federal water-quality experts predicted that the Delaware estuary would never achieve fishable water-quality standards. Until that time, the river and bay were practically open sewers for industrial and human wastes. Their polluted waters peeled paint from navy vessels, blocked the migration of fish such as shad, and created a stench bad enough to reach low-flying planes.

Thankfully, the predictions about the estuary's recovery were wrong. By 1995 the eighteen-mile-long oxygen "dead zone" on the river above and below Philadelphia was gone, and important migratory fish populations, such as shad and striped bass, were recovering. Bald eagles, whose population had dipped to one pair in the early 1980s, have now fully recovered; more than a hundred pairs nest in the estuary. The birds were once threatened by nasty chemicals such as DDT and PCBs, a chemical used in most of the hardware that delivers and makes use of electricity. But now, as the bay water gradually cleanses itself, bald eagles are thriving along the bay's fertile rivers, including Delaware's Leipsic River and New Jersey's Cohansey and Maurice rivers. The bald eagle alerted us to the dangers of chemical contamination and in the future will always act as an indicator of water quality and pollution.

The growing awareness of the bay's ecological value fueled efforts to preserve key habitats. As a result, more than 40 percent of the shoreline is now publicly owned or controlled by conservation groups. The overharvest of horseshoe crabs, and the subsequent decline of shorebirds, dominates our current perception of the bay's health. But a broader perspective highlights the tremendous conservation progress that has been achieved during the past four decades. Looking forward, though, we still face challenges that loom large for the bay. What can be done now to mitigate or prevent these threats from damaging the bay and the life that depends on it?

(Photo by Kevin T. Karlson)

Oil Spills

On May 9, 1996, the oil tanker *Anitra* spilled 40,000 gallons of its 40-million-gallon load while transferring oil to a barge at the mouth of Delaware Bay. The mostly submerged spill eventually washed ashore and significantly impacted sanderlings feeding on Delaware Bay and the Atlantic Coast. In November 2004, more than 300,000 gallons of oil spilled from the *Athos* tanker in the Delaware River. The timing of the spill spared both horseshoe crabs and shorebirds from its impact, but it underscored the constant threat that oil spills present to bay resources. However, such spills do not spare the fish and wildlife that are resident on the bay, the fish species that use the bay as a nursery, or the fish that migrate into the bay at other times of the year. Declining marsh and bay habitat for fish nurseries will have major effects on fish populations in the bay and in the Atlantic, as well as affecting both commercial and recreational fishing.

Delaware Bay is the second most important oil transport waterway in the country, second only to Galveston Bay in Texas. Measured against the amount of oil transported, Delaware Bay has the lowest spill incidence rate of the country's four major oil transport waterways, but that is cold comfort for conservationists. As long as we consume oil at current rates, spills will be a constant threat to the bay, the bay's fisheries, the shorebird stopover, and the entire bay food chain and ecosystem. Federal and state agencies must remain constantly aware and vigilant regarding these risks and hazards.

The oil tankers that come into Delaware Bay must off-load a portion of their cargo to allow them to float higher in the water so they can negotiate the channel. Pilots board the ships at the mouth to navigate up the bay to petroleum ports in Wilmington, Camden, and Philadelphia. The tankers moving through Delaware Bay are so large and heavy that it takes several miles for them to stop.

A Gulf of Mexico beach, with heavy deposits of oil from the *Deep Water Horizon* spill of 2010. At over 200 million gallons, this was the largest U.S. oil spill, nearly twenty times the amount lost from the *Exxon Valdez* in Alaska in 1989.

A sign on a Delaware beach repeats the familiar slogan to protect our wild areas, but recognizes the use of beaches by fishermen.

A severely eroded beach has left this house at Norbury's Landing exposed to storm tides and leaves less habitat for crabs and shorebirds.

Global Climate Change

Most fish and wildlife species on the bay, including shorebirds and crabs, are being significantly affected by global climate change and rising sea levels. Recent studies by the National Oceanic and Atmospheric Administration (NOAA), the New Jersey Department of Environmental Protection, and the Delaware Department of Natural Resources and Environmental Control all note the exceptional vulnerability of the bay because of its narrow mouth, which holds back outgoing tides. This increases the height of high tides, especially when winds blow into the mouth of the bay. Other effects include the ongoing subsidence of the bay's marshes and the increased precipitation in the bay watershed. Over the next ninety years, many of the bay's marshes will convert to open water, while a smaller area of low forest land and fields will convert to marsh. Overall, there will be a tremendous loss of habitat for fishery nurseries, marsh invertebrates, nesting birds, and migrant shorebirds. Many populations of invertebrates, such as fiddler crabs, will decline in direct proportion to habitat. Similarly, marsh-nesting birds, such as clapper rails and sparrows, will suffer, as will black-crowned night herons and egrets that nest in the high bushes of the marsh and feed in the tidal creeks.

Unfortunately, recent research suggests that climate change is already diminishing the prospects of full recovery of the horseshoe crab population and will very likely alter the timing of crab spawning. Even a shift of a few weeks in crab spawning would spell disaster for shorebirds, whose own timing is fixed by the narrow period of good weather in their Arctic breeding areas. New models predicting the impact on shorebird habitat are needed so conservation groups and agencies can develop new land protection strategies that incorporate the coming rise in water levels. Ultimately, the impact of climate change can only be mitigated or prevented by society at large. But any shift in breeding of horseshoe crabs will also affect a wide range of other species that depend on them.

A joint project of NOAA and the New Jersey Department of Environment Protection offers some hope in reversing the destructive influences of rising sea levels. A pilot program known as "Getting to Resilience" helps communities visualize the impact of sea-level rise to roads, historic sites, and municipal infrastructures. The program uses a geographic information system model to simulate the impact of various levels of sea level rise from one and a half to five feet for the entire bayshore. The program can be used to determine the impact on shorebird habitat and point out opportunities for moderating the impact. For example, land acquisition programs can be directed to acquire lands that will become more suitable for shorebirds, or management agencies can invest more heavily in restoring impoundments and making them more useful as shorebird roosts and feeding areas.

A bayshore road between Slaughter Beach and Mispillion Harbor, Delaware, is threatened by rising water levels.

Human Impacts on Shorebirds

Unlike other fish and wildlife in the bay, most shorebird use is concentrated into very short periods of time. Therefore anything that prevents the birds from feeding on eggs will have an impact. Researchers have found that people and dogs can keep shorebirds from foraging and cause them to lose prime foraging beaches to gulls because the gulls are less fearful of people. Managers on Delaware Bay have pioneered programs to help prevent disturbance impacts to shorebirds. In 2001, the New Jersey Division of Fish and Wildlife delineated bayshore beaches where shorebirds were most disturbed by birdwatchers, fishermen, and walkers and implemented a program to reduce these impacts. Each year, Division of Fish and Wildlife biologists train volunteer stewards to help people understand the negative effect of disturbance on shorebirds and educate them on the importance of the bay as a critical migration stopover. Stewards stationed at ten designated viewing areas give people advice on watching shorebirds and keep the sites disturbance free. They are aided by New Jersey Division of Fish and Wildlife conservation officers who are on call to help if law enforcement is necessary. Delaware Fish and Wildlife, in partnership with the DuPont company, have restored an existing building in Mispillion Harbor, Delaware, to provide the only education facility devoted to shorebirds in the country. The DuPont Nature Center at the Mispillion Harbor Reserve provides visitors with a close-up view of one of the most important stopover sites on the Delaware Bay, without disturbing the birds. The center has many displays that help educate visitors about shorebirds, their migration, and the importance of the bay as a migration stopover.

Signs encouraging people to protect migrant shorebirds are part of a New Jersey program to protect ten beaches from excessive disturbance from tourists, including photographers and birdwatchers. The birders shown here (*center and bottom*) are at a designated viewing area on a jetty at Reed's Beach, New Jersey.

Depleted Fisheries

Delaware Bay has a long history of declining and collapsed fisheries. Two species are emblematic of the problem. In the late 1800s, up to four hundred fishermen were shipping Atlantic sturgeon caviar and fish to nearby markets in New York, Philadelphia, and Baltimore. The industry was centered at a landing on Stow Creek in Salem County, New Jersey, that is still known as "Caviar Point." Sadly, overfishing and pollution reduced sturgeon numbers to the point where the population collapsed in the early 1900s, and state agencies closed the harvests. By 1985 the sturgeon population had returned to health but—under the pressure of unregulated harvests allowed by the Atlantic States Marine Fish Commission—the sturgeon were once again harvested until fishermen could not economically catch them. The Delaware Bay population now has a 50 percent chance of extinction in the next twenty years and has recently been proposed as a federally threatened species.

Weakfish also once provided steady income for Delaware baymen, and party boat captains on the bay carried thousands of people from the region on four- and eight-hour boat trips just to catch the famous sea trout. Fortescue, on the New Jersey side of Delaware Bay, was once called the "Weakfish Capital of the World" because of the large number of recreational fishermen there who caught the tasty fish, which is Delaware's

Atlantic sturgeon, which take eleven to twenty-one years to mature, can live up to sixty years of age and reach fourteen feet in length and eight hundred pounds. Sturgeon live mainly in the bay and spawn upriver between Trenton and Philadelphia. (Photo by Jay Fleming)

state fish. By the late 1990s the fishery collapsed and is now closed, probably a result of the steadily increasing harvests over the last twenty years.

The collapsed weakfish fishery was most likely another victim of overfishing. Some, however, have blamed competition with or predation by striped bass. The striped bass, itself a victim of overfishing in the 1980s, rebounded in the 2000s under very restrictive regulations that—among other controls—outlawed commercial fishing in New Jersey. Marine biologists discount the role of stripers in the decline of weakfish.

Shad, meanwhile, increased from the 1970s until 1992 because of the improving water quality in the bay and river. However, after 1992 shad numbers started decreasing, probably because of overharvest by both commercial and recreational fishermen. Fixes are now in place to increase spawning and population numbers, and to increase public awareness of the plight of shad. Fish ladders are being installed on many of the river's dammed tributaries to allow shad and other fish to move upstream to spawn.

Striped bass, one of the most popular sport fish in the Delaware Bay, were overfished to near extinction. Closed fishing seasons until the mid-1990s resulted in their spectacular recovery. (Photo by Jay Fleming)

Fishermen on Money Island off-loading their catch of oysters dredged from Delaware Bay. New Jersey's oyster fishery is centered in this small port just up the bay from Fortescue.

Below, fishermen pull in a net with American shad and gizzard shad. Pollution caused shad populations to collapse in the 1950s and 1960s, but they rebounded as water became cleaner. More recently they have declined for as yet unknown reasons. (Photo by J. Burger)

Above, eel fishermen on Delaware Bay emptying an eel trap. Horseshoe crabs are the primary bait used by eel fishermen. Eels are caught to supply the bait market for striped bass and are also shipped to Asia for food. (Photo by J. Burger)

of the harvest prior to the 1950s. Rutgers University scientists at the Cape Shore Laboratory are now experimenting with oyster cultivation along the shore of the bay near Highs Beach. These oysters, known as Cape May Salts, are creating great interest in Delaware Bay oysters and may help restore the population and oyster fishing to the bay.

Overall, hope for Delaware Bay fisheries is elusive. The bay fishery does not exist as an independent concern of marine fish agencies, so no mechanism exists for an ecosystem approach to management. An ecosystem or bay approach is being implemented by the Pacific Fisheries Management Council for 119 marine species along the West Coast, although implementation has been slow and underfunded. Ostensibly the council's focus is to manage all fisheries in a specific ecosystem to achieve broader societal goals. In Delaware Bay such an approach might result in new priorities for managing marine species for the benefit of recreational and commercial fishermen, baymen, and shorebirds and other wildlife without sacrificing the interests of the broader Atlantic Coast fishery.

If everyone can see that overharvest is bad, why does it happen over and over on the bay? The saga of the blue claw crab, an economic mainstay of baymen, illustrates the process. With the first accounts of overharvests dating back to the 1890s, wild swings in blue crab harvests are nothing new, and not uncommon. Today's annual harvest of blue crabs on the bay is estimated at about 20 million pounds, most of which is caught by commercial fishermen from both New Jersey and Delaware. The crab, unlike sturgeon and horseshoe crabs, matures and breeds in its second year of life. So it is less affected by overexploitation.

But crabs still suffer from excessive catches. Since the size of the crabs determines their price, restraints in harvests would allow crabs to reach a larger size. The minimum allowable size for blue crabs in both Maryland and Delaware is half an inch wider than in New Jersey. Not surprisingly, Maryland crabs command a better price.

The situation is a prime example of what Garrett Harding in 1968 memorably called the "tragedy of the commons." Applying the concept to crab fishing, single fishermen will always make more money by taking too many crabs, while the costs of overfishing, population collapse, and small-sized products will be shared by all fishermen, and eventually, by the fish-eating public. In this way, overwhelming harvest pressure keeps crabs small, undervalued, and ultimately vulnerable to overexploitation.

Finally, as mentioned earlier, there is the oyster. The decline in oyster numbers on the bay has been dramatic, with the harvest now a fraction

Right, researchers at the Rutgers University Cape Shore facility cultivate oysters on seven acres of intertidal flats near Villas, New Jersey, to restore the bay's oyster populations. (Photo by J. Burger)

Below, with millions harvested each year, blue crabs are the most abundantly harvested species on Delaware Bay.

Right, fishermen line the beach at Fortescue, New Jersey, the weakfish capital of the world. However, weakfish numbers have drastically declined.

Shoreline erosion threatens many bay communities. An abandoned bulkhead and remnants of a house destroyed by storms degrade beach habitat for both crabs and shorebirds (*left*).

The East Point Lighthouse, which serves as a beacon in the Maurice River cove region of the bay, is threatened by coastline erosion from severe storm tides, exacerbated by rising sea levels (*right*).

Habitat Loss and Degradation

Wildlife habitat loss in New Jersey, and to a lesser extent in Delaware, has progressed rapidly over the last twenty-five years, primarily as a result of new housing construction. But along the Delaware Bay, towns and cities have languished and some have lost population. In New Jersey, aggressive protection efforts have actually reduced the number of bayshore towns, and in both states land acquisition programs have created an expansive network of state and federal public lands and areas protected by conservation groups and shoreline regulations. Nevertheless, considerable development still takes place along the bay side of the Cape May peninsula and along much of the lower bay in Delaware.

Inside the marshes, global climate change and sea level rise have resulted in more frequent and extensive storm tides that have eroded marsh and created more areas that remain inundated, even at low tide.

The large numbers of snow geese that winter in the bay have been growing in recent years, causing some damage to the salt marsh vegetation through overgrazing. The areas denuded of vegetation have turned into mudflats that have eroded, leaving them underwater most the time. All of these changes have decreased the amount of habitat, such as mudflats and beaches, that is useful to shorebirds, and increased the amount of open water, which they don't use.

Habitat restoration projects have helped overcome some of these long-term habitat losses. Public Service Electric and Gas restored and enhanced acres of bay marsh to offset marine fish losses at the Salem Nuclear Power Plant. PSE&G's restoration projects are the most extensive, comprehensive, and diverse salt-marsh restoration projects in the nation. The project created habitats in a variety of ways, from controlling phragmites and restoring native marsh grass to returning old salt hay impoundments back to productive marsh and mudflat.

Gulls roost on an eroded sod bank (*right*) with the Salem Nuclear Power Generating Plant in the distance. A controversy over the construction of a new cooling tower resulted in the creation by the Public Service Electric and Gas Company of a landmark baywide habitat program that restored nearly 11,000 acres of *Phragmites* marsh to *Spartina* wetland and converted diked salt hay marshes to open marsh. This improved production of marine species, offsetting fish losses caused by the plant's water intake. To buffer sensitive wetlands, PSE&G also protected 21,500 acres of uplands.

A flock of red knots flies from disturbance, while the gulls remain to forage at Moores Beach. After storms and beach erosion destroyed most of the homes of this former bayshore town, during the late 1990s the State of New Jersey purchased the properties and removed the remaining dwellings.

The restored DuPont Nature Center at Mispillion, Delaware, serves as a focus for shorebird protection and restoration and offers a perfect view of horseshoe crabs and shorebirds.

PSE&G, in partnership with the N.J. Division of Fish and Wildlife, purchased all properties of one of the last towns on the New Jersey bayshore, Thompsons Beach, and partially restored it back to natural beach by removing the remaining houses in the town, many abandoned because of flooding and damaged from bay storms. Moores Beach was one of the most important beaches for spawning horseshoe crabs and shorebirds in the 1980s. After a series of severe storms, the houses that remained along the beach were partially destroyed, and the beaches migrated inward, mixing with the rubble that had protected the houses. It was therefore no longer usable for crab spawning. In the late 1990s, the N.J. Division of Fish and Wildlife and the town of Maurice River Township partnered to remove the remaining structures from the beach and partially restored the beach so that it is now one of the most important horseshoe crab spawning beaches and shorebird foraging sites.

The Delaware Department of Natural Resources and Environmental Control (DNREC) also has enhanced many places along the bay by pumping new sand onto eroding beaches in part to save communities and to improve habitat for horseshoe crabs. Spurred on by a development request for a defunct marina in Mispillion Harbor, the Delaware DNREC created protection for the shorebirds by securing development rights for land around Mispillion Harbor and creating the DuPont Nature Center.

An information sign near the Thompsons Beach restoration site, where PSE&G converted a salt hay impoundment to a natural tidal flow marsh. The company erected viewing platforms at several locations along the bay.

Horseshoe Crab Decline

For shorebirds, the number-one threat remains the tenuous recovery of the horseshoe crab population. Because the species takes at least nine years to reach breeding age, its population takes decades to recover. Today's population of shorebirds on the bay is barely a quarter of what it once was, and even at this low number, far too few of the birds reach the weight necessary to successfully breed in the Arctic. There are simply not enough eggs. Continued harvesting of the crabs will only delay the recovery of shorebirds. Because the crabs are a keystone species, recovering the horseshoe crab population as soon as possible is the first and foremost overall conservation goal for the bay.

There are number of additional threats to horseshoe crabs that, if adequately addressed, might also speed the recovery. These include loss of habitat due to bulkheading and depositing debris to combat the effect of rising sea levels. These structures trap and kill thousands of horseshoe crabs each year. These crabs could be periodically released. Righting overturned crabs could reduce mortality. Another source of mortality is a result of bleeding for the lysate industry. Estimates of mortality of bled crabs range from 15 to 30 percent. Bleeding mortality could be reduced in a variety of ways like improved handling, reducing the amount of blood taken from each crab, and returning crabs back to where they were originally captured. An additional threat comes from herring and black-backed

The harvest of horseshoe crabs has changed dramatically since the days of abundance. New Jersey banned the harvest in 2006, and, although harvesting of spawning horseshoe crabs still occurs in Delaware, quotas are much lower (*right*). Most Delaware Bay horseshoe crabs are taken by fishermen not from the bay but from ocean trawlers off the coast of Maryland and Virginia during nonbreeding periods.

gulls eating crabs overturned by bay surf, especially in storms. While this predation is natural, herring gulls did not breed in New Jersey until 1948, making them a relatively new threat. Their numbers could be reduced through better waste management procedures at landfills and resort areas.

For the last fifteen years, scientists, including the authors of this book, have conducted scientific investigations into the ecology of Delaware Bay as a stopover for migrant shorebirds. This work, including studies on movement, food habits, condition of birds, horseshoe crab egg counts, and much more, has all contributed to one of the most important databases on shorebirds in the world. Recently these data have become the cornerstone of a landmark effort by the Atlantic States Marine Fisheries Commission, U.S. Fish and Wildlife Service, U.S. Geological Survey, and four state agencies to create a mathematical model that relates red knot condition and survival with horseshoe crab population numbers. Ultimately, this model will estimate the number of crabs that can be safely harvested while still maintaining enough surplus eggs to maintain healthy shorebird populations. This ARM (Adaptive Resource Management) model is unprecedented in fisheries management and will, if successful, prevent the recurrence of the devastation caused by overharvesting. The model will simulate recovery of red knots at various horseshoe crab harvest scenarios and predict the scenario that will not cause harm and still allow a harvest. A similar model has successfully guided waterfowl harvests for the last ten years.

Above left. sea-level rise has resulted in abandonment of beach houses and other shoreline structures, leaving barriers that prevent horseshoe crabs from coming onto sandy beaches to spawn. While the eroded pilings may only impede crab breeding, the rubble dumped on the beach in the background destroys spawning habitat.

Above right. rescuing crabs may be rewarding, but it is impossible to save most of the crabs that get caught in seawalls or rubble remaining from abandoned structures.

Seawalls built to stop erosion can also prevent horseshoe crabs from coming ashore to spawn. Because the tide rises above the seawall, the crabs can end up trapped behind the wall and unable to get back to the bay. Each year thousands of crabs are killed this way around the bay.

Fishing is an important recreational pastime all around Delaware Bay. Here, men fish for weakfish or bluefish at Prime Hook, Delaware (*above*). Others catch fish or crab using small boats in tidal creeks or rivers, such as New Jersey's Maurice River (*right*). Recreational fishing is an important source of income for many Delaware bayshore businesses. Both people who fish and wildlife that depend on fish, such as this snowy egret with a small fish in its bill, have common cause in clean, productive waters (*opposite*). Although snowy egrets occur on Delaware Bay most of the year, they only breed in the upper bay on Pea Patch Island, but they also nest extensively in the nearby Atlantic coastal marshes. (Egret photo by Kevin T. Karlson)

Birdwatching is also an important recreational activity on the bay. Birders (*left*) scan shorebird flocks at Heislerville Impoundment, searching for that one rare bird among the thousands. New Jersey Audubon Society calls this impoundment a "New Jersey legend." Large flocks of shorebirds such as semipalmated sandpipers move to the impoundment to forage and roost when high tides render coastal habitats unusable (*opposite*). Birders can also witness many other species throughout the bay, including ospreys carrying fish back to their nestlings (*above*). (Osprey photo by Kevin T. Karlson)

For a few short weeks in May, the Delaware Bay is the critical link in the tenuous annual life cycles of many of the East Coast's shorebirds. Abundant horseshoe crabs make *the* difference between life and death for individual birds, for successful reproduction on their Arctic breeding grounds, and ultimately for the continued survival of these species.

For 400 million years, horseshoe crabs have endured. For at least 10,000 years their eggs have fueled the migration of red knots and other shorebirds from South America to their Arctic breeding grounds. Yet in just a decade, human shortsightedness has so decimated the horseshoe crab that this elegant relationship has unraveled. But it can be restored.

A Natural Heritage Worth Saving

Overall, the greatest problem for Delaware Bay is the overwhelming lack of recognition of its cultural heritage and natural resources. Even though the bay is recognized by international organizations such as the United Nations as a world-class natural area, it is not as ingrained in the American consciousness nearly as much as it should be. While the bay recently has suffered regrettable declines, threats such as overfishing and habitat loss are always manageable if people have the will to do so. Fish, shorebird, and horseshoe crab populations can all be nurtured back to health, and the bay can once again provide abundant opportunity for both recreational and commercial uses—but only if it is viewed as a place deserving of our attention and care.

In late May 2009, as the sun set on the Delaware Bay, the shorebird banding team watched as a significant portion of the bay's red knots and other shorebirds coalesced into small flocks and left together—hopefully for the Arctic. Having weighed many of them, the biologists knew that, for the first time in years, an increased number of these birds had gained the weight necessary to reach the Arctic and breed successfully. Flying north, the birds were carrying a lot aloft—both precious caloric fuel and the biologists' hopes that, just maybe, the birds and the ancient, elegant natural system that supports them will survive.

Index

Page numbers in *italics* indicate illustrations.

About the Authors

Lawrence Niles, Ph.D., is a scientist for the Conserve Wildlife Foundation of New Jersey. For fifteen years he served as chief of the State of New Jersey's Endangered and Nongame Species Program. He has worked for twenty-five years on red knots and other shorebirds in Delaware Bay, and has spearheaded both the scientific efforts and the conservation efforts to save the red knot and other shorebirds that have declined sharply over the last twenty years. He was the lead author on a monograph on red knots published in *Studies in Avian Biology,*  coedited *Endangered and Threatened Wildlife of New Jersey* (Rutgers University Press, 2003), and has authored many scientific papers and articles on migratory shorebirds, raptors, and wildlife conservation. He is a member of the National Shorebird Council and on the executive committee of the Western Hemisphere Shorebird Reserve Network. He and his wife, Amanda Dey, were featured in a PBS *Nature* episode on the migration of the red knots, "Crash: A Tale of Two Species." He has led expeditions to the Arctic and South America to study shorebirds for the last twelve years.

Joanna Burger, Ph.D., a Distinguished Professor of Biology at Rutgers University, has worked with shorebirds and other coastal birds in New Jersey for more than thirty-five years. Her major research has involved the intersection of avian conservation and human activities, working toward having both survive and flourish in a dense urban state like New Jersey. She has edited or authored twenty books, including *A Naturalist Along the Jersey Shore, Whispers in the Pines, Butterflies of New Jersey, 25 Nature Spectacles of New Jersey* (all Rutgers University Press), and more than four hundred scientific papers. For more than a quarter century she has

served on the New Jersey Endangered and Nongame Species Council and has served on other national and international committees. She is a recipient of the Brewster Medal from the American Ornithologists' Union, the highest award in ornithology, as well as the Conserve Wildlife Foundation of New Jersey's first Women & Wildlife Leadership Award and the Distinguished Achievement Award from the Society of Risk Analysis.

Amanda Dey, Ph.D., is a wildlife biologist for the state of New Jersey's Endangered and Nongame Species Program, and has worked for more than fifteen years on the preservation of red knots and other shorebirds on Delaware Bay. Her main research focuses on conserving and increasing populations of threatened and endangered species, ranging from neotropical migrant songbirds to shorebirds. She has published scientific papers on migratory passerines and shorebirds, including a recent

book, *Predicting Occurrence of Area-Sensitive Forest Songbirds*, based on her Ph.D. thesis. With Lawrence Niles, she was featured in a PBS *Nature* episode on the red knot and horseshoe crab, "Crash: A Tale of Two Species." She is a recipient of the Conserve Wildlife Foundation of New Jersey's Women & Wildlife Leadership Award and has been recognized by both the Littoral Society and New Jersey Audubon for her work on shorebirds on Delaware Bay.

Jan van de Kam, a Dutch wildlife photographer, has spent most of his life making pictures and films and writing books about landscapes, plants, and animals and their conservation. Recently he has focused mainly on shorebirds and their intriguing migration.

He follows them with his camera from their Arctic breeding grounds in North America and Siberia to the places where they winter. His pictures illustrate the beauty of these birds and the landscapes where they live as well as the many dangers that threaten the lives and habitats of these vulnerable creatures. His global search resulted in an illustrated book, *Invisible Connections: Why Migrating Shorebirds Need the Yellow Sea* (Wetlands International, 2008), showing the migration of shorebirds from Australia and New Zealand to Alaska and Siberia.

David Mizrahi, Ph.D., is vice president for research and monitoring for the New Jersey Audubon Society. He is the world authority on semipalmated sandpipers and has worked on this and other species in Delaware Bay for fifteen years. His research and publications focus primarily on avian migration ecology, particularly the identification of important bird stopovers and pathways with the use of radar. Recently he has led expeditions to Suriname and French Guiana to study wintering shorebirds.

Kevin Kalasz received his master's degree in applied ecology and conservation biology from Frostburg State University, Frostburg, Maryland. He has been a wildlife biologist with the Delaware Division of Fish and Wildlife's Natural Heritage and Endangered Species Program since 2001. His primary responsibilities include monitoring nongame aquatic species, marsh birds, migratory shorebirds, and oversight of the Natural Heritage Program's zoological database. Most of his time is devoted to coordinating the Delaware Shorebird Project for the conservation and protection of migratory shorebirds.

Humphrey Sitters, D.Phil., of Exeter, United Kingdom, has had a lifelong interest and commitment to bird conservation. After practicing as a lawyer for twenty-five years, he changed careers in 1990, becoming professionally qualified in ecological science (M.Sc., Aberdeen; D.Phil., Oxford) with a doctoral dissertation on the role of night feeding in shorebirds. Since graduating, Sitters has edited the *Wader Study Group Bulletin*, a shorebird science journal, and has taken a leading role in shorebird studies and related scientific publications in the United Kingdom, Australia, and the Americas. Between 1997 and 2010 he participated in thirty scientific expeditions to study shorebirds in Delaware Bay, Florida, Canada, Mexico, Brazil, Argentina, and Chile.